American
Milk and Honey

AMERICAN MILK AND HONEY

ANTISEMITISM,
THE PROMISE OF DEUTERONOMY,
AND THE TRUE ISRAEL OF GOD

DOUGLAS WILSON

CANON PRESS

MOSCOW, IDAHO

Published by Canon Press
P.O. Box 8729, Moscow, Idaho 83843
800.488.2034 | www.canonpress.com

Cover design by James Engerbretson and Josiah Nance
Interior design by Valerie Anne Bost

Unless otherwise noted, all Bible quotations are from the King James Version, public domain.

Printed in the United States of America.

Library of Congress CIP Data forthcoming

ISBN-10 1-95-790587-5
ISBN-13 978-1-957905-87-7

23 24 25 26 27 28 29 30 31 32   10 9 8 7 6 5 4 3 2

This book is for George Gilder,
for at least three or four different reasons.

Contents

Rock Wall Preface

I HAVE TO CONFESS AT THE OUTSET that this is an odd book, constructed in an odd way. There is the title for starters. And then a glance at the Table of Contents will reveal that the present writer, as the Victorians would put it, is kind of all over the road. There's a chapter on antisemitism, and one on the Talmud, and an overview of Deuteronomy, and some exegesis of Romans 11, and another chapter on the Holocaust, and a chapter on the Middle East... and it doesn't really stop there.

At the same time, these disparate chapters contain elements that are likely to be catholic in their ability to offend everybody with something, and ecumenical in their obvious affability.

Some might wonder a bit as they turn this book over in their hands. The sentiment *what the heck* might come to mind.

Perhaps this metaphor will help. I am trying to build a rock wall, one that runs in a straight line east-west, and I want it to be a dry stone wall, no mortar. These rocks have different shapes, all of them, and I want to assemble them in a way that seems coherent by the end. But until the end, you are going to have to trust me.

If you don't feel like trusting me, you can jump to the last chapter entitled "American Milk and Honey," and there you can look at the whole wall, along with a different metaphor. You won't get the detailed argumentation, but you *can* just look at the wall, and perhaps stand on it.

I confess that no one (that I know of) has built a wall quite like this before, but all the rock was honestly come by.

DOUGLAS WILSON
Yom Kippur, 2023

A Second Preface Is Almost as Good as a Second Breakfast

BEFORE ADDRESSING THE THEMES CON-
tained in this book, it would perhaps be prudent to
take a moment to orient ourselves first.

These are the times in which our secularist over-
lords are striving to impose a humanist cultural
homogenization on the entire planet, and in which
various tribes, nations, and gangs are kicking against
this through various forms of populist revolt. These
are battles of very basic allegiances—one to an ideo-
logical vision, and the other to natural and much more
local affinities.

It is our task, as members of the Christian church, to display and live out a third way, based on a yet more foundational allegiance—a loyalty to the Word of God, as over against the words of any man, whether that man is a bigwig in the World Economic Council, or some tribal chieftain. Our loyalty is to Scripture, and by "Scripture," we do not mean select passages cherry-picked and arranged in our doctrinal baskets nicely, but rather *tota et sola Scriptura*, all of Scripture and only Scripture as our ultimate and infallible rule for faith and life. Only by this means will we be able to cast down the totalitarian dreams of the one, and demote the local baals of the other. So bear with me, and wait for the surprise twist at the end.

There are two kinds of idols. One must be demolished entirely, ground into powder at the brook Kidron, and used to desecrate the graves of the people (2 Kings 23:5–7). There is to be no quarter given to this kind of idol—for example, a statue of Tash in your backyard, to which neighborhood puppies and kittens are sacrificed. That is not the sort of thing that can be gradually opposed.

But there is another kind of idol, where natural and good gifts from our heavenly Father have assumed a wrongful place in the heart loyalties of an individual. He might be greedy for money, which is idolatry (Col. 3:5), and yet after repentance he must still purchase things. He might love his father and mother in such a way as to keep him from becoming a disciple of Christ (Matt. 10:37; cf. Luke 14:26), and yet true repentance does not mean that he needs to shoot his father and mother, and bury them in a desecrated graveyard at the brook·Kidron. Rather, it means *demoting* them from the god shelf of his heart, and honoring them in the *proper* way more than he ever did in his life before.

So grace completes nature but annihilates idolatry; it absolutely destroys one kind of idol, and situates the other kind where it ought to have been all along.

We must not be children in our thinking, but rather adults. When the grace of God is poured out in reformation and revival, one of the central things that will happen is that the hearts of fathers will be turned back to their children, and the hearts of children back to their fathers (Mal. 4:5–6). Grace enables the children truly to honor their father and mother, which is the first commandment with a promise: that your life may be long in the *land* (Deut. 5:16), or *earth*, as the case may be (Eph. 6:1–3). That's an earthly blessing, right there, and it is no idol because it was grace that restored them to their proper place.

Augustine reminds us that our affections must be rightly ordered. Part of this challenge is understanding the difference between having an ultimate good in common with someone, and having a shared collection of creational goods in common with someone. If an American loves Jesus Christ as he should, then that

means he shares an ultimate good with a Chinese char-
ismatic who doesn't speak a lick of English. But the fact
that they are both going to Heaven does not alter the
fact that they would have trouble building a birdhouse
together. And an American who loves Christ might be
able to design a skyscraper with an American heathen
who worships the Marvel version of Thor. They can do
this because of all that they *do* share in common—language, training, protocols, and so on.

At the same time, our shared ultimate loyalties
might require me to smuggle a Bible to my Chinese
brother, in defiance of both his government and mine.
Our shared ultimate loyalties might require me to hide
him from persecutors who are his kinsmen or, if things
keep up the way they are going, for him to hide me
from persecutors who are mine. Paul was willing to go
to Hell for his kinsmen (Rom. 9:3), but was well aware
that they were the ones who were so ardent about killing him (Acts 23:20).

By faith, Rahab betrayed her homeland (Jos. 2:25). By
faith, Ruth abandoned her people (Ruth 1:16). By faith
Jeremiah demoralized the patriots, undermining the war
effort (Jer. 38:4). By faith Jehoiada committed treason (2
Kings 11:14–15). By faith Jonathan disobeyed his father
the king (1 Sam. 19:2). By faith David ran away from
the anointed authority (1 Sam. 19:12). They did all this
because of their ultimate loyalties, not their proximate
loyalties. Be adults in your thinking, and not children.

Some might say, in defense of their idolatrous commitment to an absolutist view of tribal identity, that Scripture tells us to stick to the bounds of our appointed habitation (Acts 17:26)—as though this exercise of God's sovereignty applied only to remote northern villages in Finland, or to White Town, Oklahoma. But God's sovereignty in this applies equally to Brooklyn, that hot pot of jumbled ethnicities.

The localist idolatries that result in poisonous attitudes like antisemitism seek to fight back against secularism with all the wrong things. We must indeed learn how to fight *for* nature, not *by means of* nature. Natural affections by themselves do not empower us to engage on behalf of nature. But anyone who cannot identify the crackle of envy in antisemitism, or the smell of sulfur that wafts off of it, is not qualified for pastoral ministry. The sheep are without a shepherd, and it is not surprising that so many are falling down crags and into crevices.

Antisemitism is one of the central themes of this book, so I thought I should define what I mean by it early on. Antisemitism is the notion that Jews are uniquely malevolent and destructive in their cultural, economic, and political influence in the world. Ethnic sin is either malicious, vainglorious, or separatist (with the desire for separation driven by either malice or vainglory), but the antisemitic forms of it usually tend toward the malicious.

It is not antisemitism to believe that Jews are sinful. This is simply orthodox Christianity. All of us are sinful. But antisemitism does believe that Jews are *uniquely* sinful, and particularly destructive. As a stand-alone dogma, this is nonsense. What plausibility it has in the minds of some can be accounted for by the fact that the Jews, as I'll argue later, are a high performance people.

One last thing, and here is your surprise twist. The mission of the Christian church is the evangelization of the entire world (Matt. 28:18–20), and the key that will unlock the global success of this effort will be the conversion of the Jews (Rom. 11:15). As we will see later, Paul argues that just as the rejection of Christ by the Jews was a great blessing for the Gentiles, so will their future acceptance of Christ be an even greater blessing.

The Pauline strategy for provoking the Jews to this repentance was for them to see all the blessings of Deuteronomy coming to pass among the Gentile nations. He wanted to provoke them to envy—a strategy that he knew would work on them. This is why we must not envy them. We must learn to live, as nations, in a way that brings down the blessings that God promised us in that glorious book of Deuteronomy.

Put simply, the key to world evangelization is the conversion of the Jews, and the key to the conversion of the Jews is Christian nationalism. Like a Russian doll.

AMERICAN MILK AND HONEY

CHAPTER 1

Antisemitism as a
False Flag Operation

ONE OF MORE DISTRESSING THINGS
that has happened over the last couple of years is that
our old equilibrium has been knocked cock-eyed.
This is certainly unsettling, but Christians can reas-
sure themselves that our sovereign God knows how
to practice creative destruction, and that He has done
this signature move often whenever a people are as
haughty as we have been. That is what we see going on
all around us now.

While trusting in His sovereign purposes, I want
to note that one aspect of our old equilibrium was the

fact that antisemitism did not have nearly the foothold here in America that it has had in Europe. This is now changing, and not in a good direction.

What's more, the antisemitism I am going to be talking about is not the central problem. It is the canary that conked out in the mine. It is the first couple of coughs in a six-month losing battle with lung cancer. It is one of the fruits of a rancid tree, the tree of envy.

ON NOT FITTING INTO ANYBODY'S SHOEBOX

Because I am going to be walking through a minefield here, I thought perhaps the best way to begin might be by strapping on a pair of snowshoes and just tromping my way across. This I propose to do by cramming a bunch of disparate facts into just one paragraph, the one immediately below this one, without taking any time to defend or explain any of them at any length. I am just putting them up to serve as the backdrop for the observations I am going to make throughout the rest of this book. It will perhaps serve the useful function of heading off some of the more predictable distortions of what I am going to say.

Quite a few members of my immediate family have significant amounts of Jewish blood in their veins. The ancestry of all my grandchildren includes Rabbi

Cohn, and for about a third of them, it also includes atheist Jews who were members of the Communist Party. I am a supersessionist, a doctrine which holds that the promises given to Israel in the Old Testament have been fulfilled in the New Israel, which is the Christian church. The Greek word *Iudaios* can be rendered either as "Jew" (as opposed to Gentiles) or as "Judean" (as opposed to Galilean), which means we really ought to revisit a number of the passages in the New Testament that talk about what "the Jews" did. At the same time, because there is no salvation apart from Christ, modern Jews who reject Christ as their Messiah are rejecting their only possible hope of salvation. I am not a Zionist, Christian or otherwise, which means I don't believe there was a *theological* case to be made for the establishment of Israel in Palestine in 1948. Nevertheless, I was not consulted, being still five years off from my natal day, and the state of Israel was established there anyhow. And like every nation on earth, now that they are established, they have every right to remain right where they are, which brings with it their right to protect themselves. I don't believe in Manifest Destiny either, but I still live in Idaho, and would take it ill if there were any general attempts at eviction. I believe that the Holocaust was a horrific evil, but I don't believe it was *sui generis*—the human race has been every bit as wicked as that before, and on numerous occasions.

So here is the challenge. When it comes to the cherry-pickers, they can go through the preceding paragraph and make me out to be a Zionist, or an antisemite, or perhaps both at the same time, whatever suits their current purposes.

I start this way because I would really like to approach this topic from what I hope is a different direction. Work with me.

THE NORMAL HUMAN CONDITION

The normal human condition, apart from Christ, is the envious condition of striving, biting, devouring, scratching, grasping, and yearning. The normal human condition is one of malice and envy. "For we ourselves also were sometimes foolish, disobedient, deceived, serving divers lusts and pleasures, *living in malice and envy*, hateful, and hating one another" (Titus 3:3; cf. 1 Pet. 2:1; Gal. 5:15).

Only the blood of Christ can liberate a man from this dismal condition, and only a widespread acceptance of a gospel ethos can render a culture *relatively* free of the pretensions and charades that envy loves to parade around in. I refer, naturally enough, to the posturing of things like "social justice." That is just a high-flying name that people give to their malevolent envy, and it is like trying to polish a turd.

Now this side of the general resurrection no culture is completely free of envy, but it is possible for a culture that is under the blessing of God to be comparatively free of it. That has been the case for much of our nation's history, but we now appear to be in the middle of a wholesale rejection of that particular blessing. I mean, look at us. Our current events are being driven by economic envy (socialism), racial envy (BLM), sexual envy (feminism), and so on. The real rot in all of this is that our ruling elites have no coherent response because the spirit of envy has them by the throat as well. Our unregenerate streets are full of envy and rage. There was a time when it was not this way.

But it stands to reason. Apart from Christ, the electric crackle of envy runs along *all* the wires. Everything is hooked up to this particular grid. The current flows from Gentile to Jew, Jew to Gentile, white to black, black to white, short to tall, fat to skinny, and so on—mimetic desire and carping envy are absolutely everywhere and in everything. People who dismiss this with a wave of the hand do not understand the Scriptures, and they are blind when it comes to identifying one of the mainsprings of all unregenerate human action. The prohibition of envy and covetousness ("of *anything* that is your neighbor's") is in the Ten Commandments for a reason.

So much wealth. So much wickedness. So much guilt. So many disparities. So many lies. So much stupidity. So little gospel. Of *course* we are at each other's throats.

Given the fact that this sin is everywhere, it also stands to reason that it is right at the center of Gentile-Jew relations. Paul was very aware of it, and describes it as jealousy and emulation.

> But I say, Did not Israel know? First Moses saith,
> I will provoke you to jealousy by them that are no
> people, and by a foolish nation I will anger you.
> (Rom. 10:19)

> I say then, Have they stumbled that they should
> fall? God forbid: but rather through their fall sal-
> vation is come unto the Gentiles, for to provoke
> them to jealousy. (Rom. 11:11).

> If by any means I may provoke to emulation them
> which are my flesh, and might save some of them.
> (Rom. 11:14).

Now when violence erupts between different ethnic groups, it is not just because of something so simple and straightforward as a different skin tone, or bone structure, or facial features. For many people, it is easy to assume that all such ethnic disputes are the result of nothing more than the star-bellied sneetches being rude to those without stars. But one of the things we need to learn how to do here is *follow the money*. Ethnic clashes often have a strong economic component to them, and these economic components are frequently tangled up with envy. The economic component is not a superficial thing at all—despite the efforts of many to reduce everything to surface issues like skin tint.

We see this in many places. This has been a factor in the Catholic/Protestant violence in Northern Ireland, with the Protestants being the wealthier class. It has been a player in the persecution that the Chinese have suffered in places like Malaysia. The Chinese there are only about 5 percent of the population, but they work like crazy and run three-quarters of the nation's top businesses. This is something people notice, and it has resulted in more than a few conflicts.[1] In such cases, those who resort to violence are "punching up" at those they regard as their economic oppressors.

But it can also happen, for *economic* reasons, if people are feeling crowded or threatened from below. This is what happened in the Tulsa Race Massacre in 1921, when a wealthy black district in Tulsa was essentially burned to the ground and hundreds were murdered by rioting whites. Money always talks.

And money has often been an issue when it comes to justifications of antisemitism. Just think of all the tropes representing the greedy Jews, the Shylocks, the bankers of Zion. If you leave envy out of it, you are

1. George Gilder, *The Israel Test* (New York: Richard Vigilante Books, 2009), 37.

trying to understand a world that runs on envy without any reference to envy.

In two places Paul puts malice and envy cheek by jowl (Rom. 1:28–29; Titus 3:3), and this is no accident. In the Bible, whenever envy moves, violence and coercion are not far off (Acts 7:9; 13:45; 17:5; Matt. 27:18). Envy sharpens its teeth every night.

This is the natural condition of man, Jews and Gentiles both. It is a universal problem. Before we were converted, Paul says we were "foolish, disobedient, deceived, serving divers lusts and pleasures, living in malice and envy, hateful, and hating one another" (Titus 3:3). Even when we are brought into Christ, this does not grant us automatic immunity to this sin—we must still guard ourselves. For example, the godly have to be told not to envy sinners (Prov. 3:29–32; 23:17–18).

Envy is the invisible vice. In striking contrast to many other sins, nobody readily admits to being envious. Envy is petty and malicious. Envy is unattractive to just about everybody, and in order to operate openly in the world, it has to sail under false colors. Envy is clandestine; envy is sneaky. To admit to envy is to admit self-consciously to being tiny-souled, beef jerky-hearted, petty, and mean-spirited—and to *admit* this is dangerously close to repentance. To be out-and-out envious is to be clearly in the wrong, to confess yourself to be an inferior.

Recognizing our complicity in the sin is the way of escape. That recognition is called repentance, and can only be found in Christ.

Our modern political tangles are a veritable festival of envy, everywhere you look. Trying to find envy in our political disputes—and especially when it involves the Jews—is like trying to find some beads at the New Orleans Mardi Gras parade.

In stark contrast to all of this, the apostle Paul said, "Love does not envy" (1 Cor. 13:4). And the reason love does not envy is because love was crucified on the cross, and love was sent to that cross because of envy, as Pilate recognized (Matt. 27:18). And then love rose from the dead, leaving all that envy behind in the grave.

RIGHT-WING RAGE PORN AND THE JEWS

The ancients rightly said that anger is a brief madness. And when anger and rage settle into the bones, it is best to drop the *brief*, and simply call it madness. Another way of saying it is that anger doesn't see straight. It is hard to see straight and see red at the same time.

One of the things I see developing on the Right in this regard is extremely worrisome, and it is a whole lot bigger than just the Jewish question. The issue of rising antisemitism is just a piece of it—but I want to argue it is a revelatory piece nonetheless. One of the oddities of the current turmoil is how certain sectors of the alt-right have, on the issue of Israel and the Jews, become a mirrored counterpart of the raging antisemitism of the left. How did it come about that such disparate groups would agree on something like that?

Envy is the fuel that the left has always run on, and so much is a matter of course. On the right, the recent populist uprising against conservative leaders who don't believe in conserving much of anything has accomplished a lot of good. But one of the vulnerabilities it has created (a vulnerability that is becoming increasingly apparent by the day) is that it has made some on the right susceptible to the seductive allurements of envy—outsiders against insiders, little guys against big guys, deplorables against the omnicompetent Bond villains, *goyim* against the Jewish cabal, and so on.

It is a trap. It is a squirrel cage run. This book was written to help you get off it now.

This is why some conservatives need to stop eating their anger porridge every morning. I am not sure how this came about, but a number of the algorithm gremlins have somehow decided that I am a fitting target for various forms of what might be called right wing rage spam. As a result, on a daily basis, multiple times a day, I am cordially invited to see Senator So-and-so drop a BOMB on AOC, or to watch as an angry mom OBLITERATES a school board somewhere, or to click on something that will enable me to observe a Texas sheriff WIPE THE FLOOR with some ding dong at CNN. It has to be acknowledged that a lot of people on the right appear to *like* hating.

Now for those who have been around the kind of things I write, you will know that I believe we are supposed to have enemies. And I also believe it is most necessary that we fight them. At the same time, and this cannot be emphasized too much, we are under the strictest of orders to *love* our enemies (Matt. 5:44; Luke 6:27, 35). Love is not inconsistent with a vigorous polemic. It is not inconsistent with prophetic rhetoric. It *is* inconsistent with scurrilous abuse. "And peace, Eustace. Do not scold, like a kitchen-girl."

When envy has metastasized, and gotten to a certain point, it is impossible to hide—kind of like Shylock's nose. And one of the very first things it wants to do is to draw Shylock's nose like that.

A HIGH PERFORMANCE PEOPLE

The Jews are a high-performance people. This means that when they are good, they are very, very good, and when they are bad, they can really be awful.

One high-talent Jew cooks up a cancerous Marxist plague that emanates from the Frankfurt School, a guy with a name like Horkheimer, say, and another high-talent Jew carves out a cure for cancer from a bar of soap, with a name like Horowitz, say, thus winning the Nobel Prize—his third. Because the first guy is malevolent, the destructive impact of his high-talent malevolence is high. Bad things happen all over the world as a result. We are looking at you, George Soros. Because the second guy is pursuing his own glory, not the glory of God, he already has his reward (Matt. 6:2), not yet having learned that a man who gives everything he has to the poor without love is still nothing (1 Cor. 13:3). But we still have the cure for cancer, for which we thank God.

What antisemites want to do is point to the outsized Jewish involvement in things that really are nefarious, or in things considered by them to be nefarious. What they overlook is the outsized Jewish involvement in things that are helpful, wholesome, and good. The knee-jerk antisemite won't acknowledge the outsized contribution to things that are helpful to society, just as the knee-jerk philosemite won't acknowledge how many of the early Bolsheviks were Jews, thus ushering in a century of bone-grinding misery for millions of people. This section is devoted to an acknowledgment of the positive contributions, without denying that there is a negative side as well.

George Gilder gave us this summary.

Today tiny Israel, with its population of 7.23 million, five and one-half million Jewish, stands behind only the United States in technological contributions. In per-capita innovation, Israel dwarfs all nations.... As one of the world's most profitable economies built on one of the world's most barren territories, Israel challenges all the materialist superstitions of zero-sum economics.[2]

One of the things that our egalitarian age has insisted upon is that we treat everyone as standing shoulder-to-shoulder on this thing that we like to call the "level playing field." It is a dogma of our generation, not to be challenged, that everybody is basically the same.

The problem is that everybody isn't the same. This makes inadvertent contact with data pretty awkward, and when we encounter some facts, we don't know which way to look.

According to Charles Murray, author of *The Bell Curve*, "The key indicator for predicting exceptional accomplishment (like winning a Nobel Prize) is the incidence of exceptional intelligence.... The proportion of Jews with IQs of 140 or higher is somewhere around six times the proportion of everyone else."[3]

This results in outsized performance any way you look at it. According to Murray's calculations in his subsequent book *Human Accomplishment*, the Jewish population of the world is about three-tenths of 1

2. Gilder, *The Israel Test*, 4–7.
3. Ibid., 33.

percent of the world's population, and is responsible for about 25 percent of "recent notable human-intellectual accomplishment in the modern period."[4]

In the second half of the twentieth century, the percentage of Nobel Prizes that went to Jews was 29 percent. As the twenty-first century began, it was higher than that.[5]

Now if the dogma of egalitarianism has you by the throat, when confronted with hard statistics like this, your only explanation is that the Jews must be *cheating*. And so, with a very convenient maneuver, Jewish crimes can be blamed on the Jews and Jewish accomplishments can be blamed on the Jews also—on their ability to rig the system dishonestly. Jewish mothers are apparently pestering Nobel officials both near and far.

But then you discover that they win 51 percent of the Wolf Foundation Prizes in Physics, 28 percent of the Max Planck Medailles, 38 percent of the Dirac Medals for Theoretical Physics, 37 percent of the Heineman Prizes for Mathematical Physics, and 53 percent of the Enrico Fermi Awards.[6] *Fiends*, I tell you.

The attitude that will not brook this kind of manifest superiority is, to be blunt, a carping and critical spirit of envy. As Thomas Sowell once put it memorably, the one thing the Jews could do that would put all

4. Gilder, *The Israel Test*, 34.

5. Ibid., 34–35.

6. Ibid., 35.

this envy to rest would be, and I quote, "Fail." As long as they continue to succeed as they have the clear tendency to do, they will continue to draw the ire of those who absolutely hate being surpassed in this way.

As I have said before, envy is one of those sins that nobody is proud of because nobody likes acknowledging the inferior position that makes an envious reaction seem plausible. And as a consequence, I have seen many antisemites hotly deny that they are motivated by envy at all. But if they had put just a fraction of the energy into starting a small business that they instead expended on studying the malfeasance of Jews I have never heard of, they could be looking at an early retirement by now.

Now I have been throwing around insensitive terms like "superiority" and "inferiority," and so I should take a moment to explain that. I am not talking about any kind of innate genetic superiority, the kind that racialist theorists like to fantasize about. I am talking about a particular kind of *cultural* superiority, drilled into Jews over the course of centuries. I am talking about things like shared worldview, tight family cohesion, disciplined dedication to a text outside themselves, a hard commitment to accomplishment, and related issues. When we talk about superiority, we are talking about human cultural behavior, and not the behavior of our DNA.

When Murray published his book *The Bell Curve*, cited earlier, there was an uproar. The reason for this is that he was comparing the IQ scores of various ethnic groups, and those scores did not look like a flat, straight line. Whites outscored blacks, and Asians outscored whites, and you can see what this would do to any worldview that was allergic to things like facts.[7]

One of the things that made the controversy misleading was that certain assumptions were being made about IQ being a hard-wired sort of thing. The scores are just the scores, but there is something called the Flynn Effect, named after a gentleman who was peeved by the sort of thing that Murray reported, and who dug into it a little more deeply. What many people don't realize is that IQ tests are periodically re-normed. The median and mean of an IQ test are both 100, with most people averaging a score within 15 points of that either way—between 85 and 115. If people start gradually scoring higher on the tests, at some point they will have to re-norm the test, in order to bring the center back to 100. When these adjustments to the test are taken into account, you discover that a genius score in the 1920s amounts to a below-average score today.[8] In other words, we are not talking about a fixed *biological* superiority or inferiority. We are talking about things like religion, culture, education, family, economics, and so on.

7. Charles Murray, *The Bell Curve* (New York: The Free Press, 1994), 269–315.
8. Steven Johnson, *Everything Bad Is Good for You* (New York: Riverhead Books, 2006), 139–143.

THE PAULINE STRATEGY

Interestingly, the apostle Paul puts a godly use of envy right at the center of his strategy for evangelizing Jews. And what I am urging here means that antisemitism among professing Christians is a photo negative of that strategy. It is about as unbiblical as you can get. It fuses two of the worst traits of human beings: malevolence and stupidity.

Paul's strategy is to provoke the Jews to envy us. We are not supposed to envy them.

> I say then, Have they stumbled that they should fall? God forbid: but rather through their fall salvation is come unto the Gentiles, for *to provoke them to jealousy.* (Rom. 11:11)

> . . . if by any means I may *provoke to emulation* them which are my flesh, and might save some of them. (Rom. 11:14)

I believe that Paul is playing the long game here. It is not just a matter of personal salvation and forgiveness and relief, although all of that is right at the foundation. We are actually talking about the blessings of *Deuteronomy* coming to the *Gentile* nations that have received the Messiah of the Jews. These Gentile nations will consequently become the head, and not the tail, and Paul knew that this was a strategy that would actually work on his people.

Carping envy from Gentiles only reinforces Jewish unbelief. It feeds and nourishes Jewish unbelief. It is a central complicating part of the problem of Jewish unbelief. It is an envy that feeds the drivenness of the excluded Jew. It is like Harold Abrahams in that great film *Chariots of Fire.* He was an unbelieving Jew who was so driven that he wanted "to take them all on, one by one, and run them off their feet." The Christian in the film, Eric Liddell, brought the real answer. He simply wanted to run because he "feels God's pleasure." Grace can run fast too. Incidentally, one of the most powerful and understated moments in the film is right at the end, when you realize that the funeral of Harold Abrahams is a *Christian* funeral.

The very best thing we can do for the Jewish people is labor to build a Christian culture that runs the way Eric Liddell ran—under the pleasure of God.

CHAPTER 2
The Holocaust

FOR VARIOUS REASONS, THE BACKDROP of the Holocaust has made conversation about the issues addressed in this book extraordinarily difficult. The Holocaust was, as we all know, horrific. But for those who understand the kind of world Scripture teaches we actually live in, it was not *uniquely* horrific. So to keep the rest of this book in perspective, we need to say something about the place of the Holocaust in our thinking.

Because we live in a time when victimhood confers power, a lot of our politics is taken up with a scramble for that victim status. This in no way denies the grim reality of genuine victimization, which obviously happens, sometimes at true genocidal levels. It is simply to note that when there are perks for those recognized as survivors, and those perks are being handed out, not all the people who get in line are doing so out of the goodness of their hearts. Some of this happens as a result of simple confusion, but in other instances the motives are more mercenary.

Over time, movements tend to turn into rackets. There is such a thing as the Holocaust hustle. People assume the only way to drive home the point of "never again" is to convince everyone that the Holocaust was *uniquely* evil, not simply *evil*, and this requires the imposition of a particular narrative. When that happens, facts don't matter, and you are just a few steps away from a hustle.

But while some have a vested interest in the Holocaust's uniqueness, there are others who have a vested interest in the opposite direction. They want to say that the Holocaust didn't happen at all. Everywhere you go, you run into people.

We have been warned that if we dare to "minimize" something like the Holocaust "in any way," we are either Holocaust deniers, or we are enabling Holocaust deniers. Now of course there is a way to minimize the horror that really amounts to Holocaust denial, and nobody should even think about doing that. But to point out that there have been other atrocities in history, every bit as horrendous, is not to minimize the horror. What it does is frame the question the way it ought to be framed—in terms of *human* wickedness. This is quite different from framing it in terms of a unique Gentile wickedness, which finally came to fruition after centuries of slowly metastasizing.

So there is actually another route to Holocaust denial. It is to make wild and unsupportable claims, and then to flay anyone who questions those wild claims. This causes a certain kind of simpleton to reason that he might as well be hanged for a sheep as for a lamb, and so he starts to deny the whole thing, top to bottom.

A judicious Christian take on the Holocaust should be that it was Hitler's ugly and genocidal attempt at a final solution to his "Jewish problem," one that resulted in murder on a staggering scale. Christians should never defend the indefensible, and this human tragedy would be among the great indefensible things. But this dark episode must be placed alongside any number of other atrocities—the kind of atrocity that is tragically characteristic of human history. This is the sort of thing we periodically do, and with some regularity.

George Gilder, an enthusiastic friend of Israel if ever there was one, said it this way:

> It is unseemly, as well as tactically questionable,
> for American Jews, the richest people on earth,
> to grapple with Armenians and Rwandan Tutsis,

> Palestinian Arabs and U.S. blacks, Sudanese,
> and American Indians to corner the trump card
> of victimization. . . . Every ethnic group has its
> own tale of woe, because the entire history of the
> world is woebegone.[1]

I agree with this entirely. We could talk about the eradication of about a quarter of the population of Cambodia over the course of four years under the communist Khmer Rouge—somewhere between 1.5 million and 3 million people were slaughtered then. Or perhaps we could talk about Tamerlane who, after conquering a city that resisted him, would leave behind a pyramid made up of 70,000 to 90,000 human skulls. Or the 2 million dead as a result of the Middle Passage of the Atlantic slave trade. Or the three years of the Armenian genocide, in which between 1.2 and 1.5 million Armenians were slaughtered by the Turks.

Despite what some might say, to give a long list of crimes like this is not to flatten or relativize the Holocaust. But it does do something important. It places the Holocaust firmly within a Christian narrative of the world. And if the Christian faith is *true*, then that is where it belongs. Confronted with something as awful as the Holocaust, we are forced to ask what it *means*. For the Christian, it means that the

1. Gilder, *The Israel Test*, 39–40.

human race is desperately fallen, broken, and wicked, and is in need of the forgiveness that only Christ can bring—to the Jew first, and also to the Greek. For the Jew who wants the Holocaust to be treated as *absolutely* unique, and not ever to be compared with other historical events, what the Holocaust means is either that the Jews themselves are absolutely unique, or that Gentiles are uniquely evil, or a combination of the two. Neither of these are options for consistent Christians.

In this latter view, antisemitism was a disease of the Gentile mind, running back centuries, leading to pogrom upon pogrom, and finally culminating in the ultimate Pogrom. The memory of this grotesque event must be sacralized, and the Jewish people must get "never again" down into their bones. The cry of "never again" is a good one, obviously, but we want to make sure we get the reasons for it straight. As Solzhenitsyn once put it, the line between good and evil runs down the middle of every human heart. To draw the line between black and white, or Jew and Gentile, or male and female, is to misplace the antithesis.

In other words, history can be a complicated mess. The antithesis between good and evil isn't tidy. It is a mixed bag everywhere you look.

For example, the First Crusade was accompanied by an outbreak of antisemitism, some of it motivated by a desire to fund the Crusade. But what many don't realize is that the Church hierarchy condemned these attacks on the Jews, and gave refuge to a number of them. Gregory X and Benedict XIII both said that Jews were not the enemies of Christians and that the lives and properties of Jews were to be respected.

When the Black Death broke out, the Jews were scapegoated and accused of being behind the plague by means of well-poisoning, and a number of atrocities were committed against them. For example, in Strasbourg, about 900 Jews were herded into a synagogue which was then burned to the ground. But in this moment of crisis, a number of bishops gave refuge to Jews in their homes. Pope Clement VI issued two papal bulls that refuted the idea of well-poisoning. He also pointed out that Jews were dying of the plague also, which would seem to be relevant.[2]

The fact remains that many who called themselves Christians engaged in atrocious behavior against the Jews. But the perpetrators of these crimes did not commit them because they were Gentiles. They committed them because they were sinners, descended from Adam. The problem turns out to be *people*. And because Jews are also people, they have also had their turn.

For example, in the seventh century, the Jews of Babylon were major players in the Middle East: "There, within the Persian Empire, they had their

---

2. John Stonestreet and Glenn Sunshine, "The Church and Antisemitism," *Breakpoint*, 2 January 2023, https://www.breakpoint.org/when-the-church-has-opposed-antisemitism.

own tongue and currency, their own laws and army. In fact, for more than a thousand years, they formed an independent state within the Mesopotamian ruling power."[3]

A Judean-Persian army attacked Byzantine cities and succeeded in conquering Antioch. The patriarch there, Anastasius, was castrated and disemboweled, had his intestines and genitals stuffed in his mouth, and was dragged, still alive, through the city streets. After a three-week siege, these forces captured Jerusalem with a lot of bloodshed, and burned down the Church of the Holy Sepulcher, along with all the people who took refuge there.[4]

The problem, again, was not the Jewish "race" but rather the human race.

We need to engage with antisemites over the sheer fact of the Nazi atrocities against the Jews. That genocide and attempt at complete genocide really did happen. But we also must debate the meaning of the Holocaust with the Jews. It does not mean what many Christ-rejecting Jews are claiming it means. If Christ rose from the dead, it cannot mean that.

3. David Mitchell, *Messiah ben Joseph* (Glasgow: Campbell Productions, 2016), 154.
4. Ibid., 154–156.

CHAPTER 3

Hot Mess in the Middle East

QUITE ASIDE FROM WHETHER OR NOT the establishment of Israel as a state in the Middle East was a good idea to begin with, it was an idea that actually got implemented, and consequently millions of Israeli citizens live there. Wanting to make things better now is not a utopian pipe dream, but in order to make things better, we need a rudimentary understanding of how we got in this position in the first place. We do not do this in the vain hope that we might somehow unring the bell, but rather so that we might look at the Middle East stalemate a bit more objectively—even if being objective means looking like you are taking sides, which it sometimes will.

The ongoing turmoil in the region is usually treated as the most intractable problem in the world, and it is, but this is not the same thing as the most complicated problem in the world. The problem is intractable because the hatred for Israel is intractable—but the hatred is pretty simple to understand. That part is not complicated.

A BRIEF HISTORY OF MODERN ISRAEL

Let's review. The state of Israel was established in 1948. The way that this happened was particularly galling to the Muslim world. A big part of the hostility toward Israel is directed at Israel directly—a hostility toward Jews as Jews. But quite a bit of it is indirect and is present because of resentment of the Christian West—and there is a long history there. Now for sincere Christians in the West today, we are well aware how far short of biblical standards we fall, and so calling ourselves "the Christian West" kind of sticks in the throat. If we have read the Sermon on the Mount recently, it ought to stick in the throat. But fundamentalist Muslims are not nearly so fastidious about religious demarcations, and they see the clash between their values and ours as a religious clash. And at the baseline level, I would argue they are correct in this assessment. So let us go into that history a bit.

In the century after the death of Muhammad, the great Muslim conquest of the Mediterranean world basically turned that sea into a Muslim lake. It was a conquest that lined up perfectly with the revelations that had been given to their prophet. What the Koran said they were supposed to be doing, they *were* doing, and Allah appeared to be giving them great success. The high-water mark of their expansion was at the Battle of Tours, when Charles Martel finally halted their imperialistic growth in AD 732. This stopped them from going any further, but they could be excused for thinking that their theology of conquest and their actual conquests were still lining up pretty well. They certainly had a strong hand, which they played *as* a strong hand for a long time.

All of this continued for some centuries, with interruptions from the Crusades and things like that, but the first signs of real trouble for the Islamic hegemony were three battles: Malta (AD 1565), Lepanto (AD 1571), and Vienna (AD 1683). A close observer of those developments should have turned to the sultan and said something along the lines of *uh oh*. But a lot of the external solidity was still impressive, so no one took serious notice.

Now I trust that the reader understands that I am flying over all of this material at 30,000 feet, and there is a certain amount of *skipping, skipping, skipping* going on, but one of the great manifestations of this Islamic power was the Ottoman Empire, centered in what is now Turkey. This empire lasted for 600 years,

down to *1922*. This was just four years after the close
of World War I. The reason this matters is that after
the close of the Great War, the Western powers walked
into the Middle East and carved the whole thing up
like it was a pie.

And during the course of the war, in 1917, Britain
issued the Balfour Declaration, supporting a Jewish
homeland in Palestine. At the time, Palestine was
under the Ottomans, and had a little teeny Jewish population. After the war, Jews started to immigrate there,
and it wasn't long before there was trouble between
them and the locals. But in my judgment, while part of
this was caused by the presence of the Jews, a particularly galling aspect of it was the fact that the Christian
powers were walking around like they owned the
place, which they kind of now did.

Think of the Jews as a foster child that the authorities placed in your home, and you and the foster child
didn't hit it off very well, and you aren't getting along.
So there's that. Couple this with the fact that you never
signed up for the foster child program in the first place,
and that the Christian West, the placement authorities
in this little parable, just showed up with the kid one
day. Then, to make things a little more festive, let us suppose that the new foster kid started outperforming all
your biological kids—kept his room clean, kept his bed
made, pulled down straight A's, received multiple hon-
ors scholarship offers, then won the Nobel Prize, and

so on. In addition, just to keep the illustration on the realistic side, we should also recognize that the foster child was capable of misbehaving—like the paramilitary campaign conducted by Zionists against the British from 1944 to 1948. Some of the other kids remember the bombing of the King David Hotel, for example. That was the time when the West was trying to *not* place the foster kid there, and the foster kid was fighting to stay. But if we press it any further, our analogy will run away from us, just like one of the kids might.

In this scenario, a lot of the anger is going to be taken out on Israel, because they are located right *there*. But the deepest animus is toward the entire West who caused all this, and who shouldn't have ever been in a position to cause anything like it. If someone were to say that this doesn't make sense because we haven't done *that* many bad things to them, this misses the point. We are talking about affronted pride and wounded envy. The Christian West (in Muslim eyes) is enjoying the kind of superior firepower and material wealth that Muslims should be enjoying—that is, what they would be enjoying if they had not angered Allah somehow. This whole set up is a standing crisis of faith for the devout Muslim. The terrorism and ill-fated wars are not an indication of a confident zeal, true dedication, and vibrant faith. It is more like panic and flailing just before you drown. It is like the kamikaze flights near the end of the Second World War.

So we come back to the period between the two
world wars. Events kept eventing, as they are wont
to do, and after a time there was a significant Jewish
population there. The year before Israel became a
nation, in 1947, the United Nations voted to partition Palestine into two states, a Jewish state and an
Arab state. The Jews accepted this partition, while
all the surrounding Arabs rejected it. So the day after
British rule there ended, a bunch of the surrounding nations—Lebanon, Iraq, Transjordan, Syria, and
Egypt—attacked Israel in order to destroy it. That
attack failed, and Israel survived.

Almost twenty years later, the 1967 war erupted.
Egypt's dictator, Gamal Abdel Nassar, said that he
was going to "destroy Israel," and massed troops on
the border. Syria did the same, and Israel responded
with a preemptive attack on both Egypt and Syria, and
pleaded with Jordan not to enter the war. But Jordan
entered the war anyway, in which Israel was victorious.
This is how Israel wound up with control of Jordanian
land on the western side of the Jordan River, in what
is now called the West Bank.

Shortly after that war, the Arab states gathered in
Khartoum, and issued their "Three No's"—no recognition, no peace, and no negotiations. If we were to
reduce it all to one "No," it would be, *no way*.

But in 1978, because Egypt had come under new
leadership, Israel gave the Sinai Peninsula (along with

its oil) back to Egypt. They had conquered that land (bigger than the nation of Israel itself) in the '67 war. They gave this land back, in exchange for a statement of Israel's right to exist as a nation.

And Israel has always been willing to do the same thing with the Palestinians. In the year 2000, they offered the Palestinians their own state, including Gaza and 95 percent of the West Bank. But the Palestinian leadership rejected the offer, and sent waves of terrorists into Israel.

Dennis Prager once laid out an interesting thought experiment about all this. Suppose one day Israel just laid down their arms and announced that they would fight no more, no matter what. What would happen? It is not hard to envision. Israel would be wiped out. And then flip the thought experiment around. Suppose all the Arab states around Israel just laid down their arms one day and announced that they would fight no more, no matter what. Now what would happen? In the first scenario, it would result in the destruction of Israel, and the slaughter of her population. In the second scenario, it would result in Middle East peace.

Now the outline I have just given seems pretty simple, and wars are always messier than that. Many Palestinians were displaced in the 1948 war, and then the West Bank came under Israel's control in the 1967 war. These Palestinians really have been displaced, or made to live in occupied territory—but who is responsible for this? How did it happen? The West Bank was occupied by Israel in the '67 war. But who started that war? It would appear to me that the Palestinian leadership holds that responsibility. They could have a Palestinian state *tomorrow* (not counting Jordan, which already *is* a Palestinian state) if they would simply acknowledge Israel's right to exist, and agree to live in peace.

Like I said, an objective account looks like it is taking sides.

WHAT IS TERRORISM?

When we consider the armed conflicts that break out in Israel from time to time, it is very easy for critics of Israel, *some* of whom are antisemitic, to simply assert that Israel is guilty of terrorist atrocities, and that the ongoing conflict will not end until this is stopped.

It is also very easy, but quite simplistic, to say that terrorism is "what the big army calls the little army." The word *terrorism* refers to a tactic, and *terrorist* should never be used as a synonym for enemy, or evildoer, or person with whom you have had a sharp political disagreement. We are not going to get very far in discussions about the perennial impasse in the Middle East unless we define—and define consistently—what we mean by terrorism exactly. The way I am using it here, terrorism refers to military forces (guerrilla or regular units) making war directly on civilian targets that have no direct military value, and doing so for the purpose of demoralizing the entire population of the enemy nation.

Terrorism is therefore in the same category with *surprise attacks*. It is a tactic, and in order for this particular tactic to work, it needs to be open and avowed. Terrorism is a threat from a particular group, saying that if the demands are not met, then everyone can expect more of the same from that group. In order to drive toward fulfillment of those demands, the victims of the attacks need to know what their demands are, and that means they need to know who is responsible. That is why terrorist groups frequently "claim responsibility" after an attack.

So when one military force engages with another one, this is war, not terrorism. When one military force attacks a target with military significance (say, a munitions factory), and the majority of those killed are civilian workers in that factory, this is war, not terrorism. When one military force attacks that munitions factory, and some civilians who live next door to the factory are killed, this is collateral damage, a feature of war, and not terrorism. If the intelligence forces discovered that all the workers in the factory dropped their kids off at a school and day care center on the other side of the city, and they bombed *that* in order to demoralize the workers, that would be terrorism. In such a case war is being waged on civilians and non-combatants for the sole purpose of generating terror.

It is easy for pacifists to sniff at phrases like "collateral damage," as though the death and suffering of any civilians is simply inexcusable, but this cannot be sustained biblically. In the ancient world, there was no clean way to separate combatants from non-combatants. When you besieged a city, the entire city was besieged and not just the soldiers. The law of God assumes that Israel would go to war and that sieges would be part of what they would do. It was one of the legitimate tactics in their range of options.

> When thou shalt besiege a city a long time, in
> making war against it to take it, thou shalt not
> destroy the trees thereof by forcing an axe against
> them: for thou mayest eat of them, and thou
> shalt not cut them down (for the tree of the field
> is man's life) to employ them in the siege. (Deut.
> 20:19).

When a city was besieged, there was no way to keep the women and children from suffering, and with many of them dying. But when this happened, it was collateral damage and not the central point. A righteous army would prefer to engage with enemy armies in the field.

So with that understanding in hand, let's go on to
talk about Israel and Hamas. What we say will have
applications to other conflicts, obviously, but these
two will do as placeholders. What we must learn to
do is distinguish between an Israeli military opera-
tion which works hard to avoid civilian deaths and an
attack by Hamas, which has often targeted civilians
directly. The issue is *not* whether civilians die. The
issue is whether this particular tactic is being used.

As stated earlier, Jesus Christ is the only hope of
every nation, and this includes Israel. This means that
Muslims and Israelis are both summoned in the gospel
to surrender to Jesus Christ, and until that happens,
there will never be lasting peace between them. How
could there be? That is the first thing.

Second, we can acknowledge that this particular mess in the Middle East would not be occurring
if it had not been for the misbegotten policies of the
Zionism of yesteryear. Israel had no peculiar divine
right to that territory, but they went there anyway, and
bad things started to happen because Zionism as a
doctrine was not a good idea. But in just the same way,
Manifest Destiny was a piece of impudence cooked
up by Americans during our "look at us go" stage. I
don't hold to the doctrine of Manifest Destiny *at all*,
along with the assumptions that were underneath it.
And yet, here my house is, ensconced in Idaho, right
in the middle of Manifest Destiny territory. I own that

house, have a legitimate right to it, and would object in quite forceful terms if Nez Perce Indians were shooting rockets at it.

No international policy that demands that every people group return to their original homeland of, say, three thousand years ago, can lay any claim to moral seriousness at all. And ironically, if we began making that kind of demand, the Israelis would suddenly have a much stronger claim on their land ... at least until the Amorites showed up anyway.

This is why Israel has every right to defend themselves against rocket attacks. In order to make this observation, it is not necessary to enter into the inner councils of whichever conspirators you believe are actually running the world. All you have to do is look at what the two sides are *publicly* doing or saying, and think about it carefully for a minute.

Hamas, hopelessly outgunned and outnumbered, can nevertheless successfully provoke Israel into a military response. "No response" on the part of Israel would clearly be impossible, and yet a military response puts them into the role, on the international stage, of kicking puppies. This is because Hamas can position themselves in such a way as to make it impossible for a military response to not hit civilians, and a lot of them. In this case, military weakness is PR strength, just so long as you have sentimentalists there with cameras. So if you want to understand what is going on, you have to know how to look past the spin war. I can see on camera which side is shooting rockets, and which side is driving the tanks. But which side is pointing the cameras? Christians should be a little more suspicious of the direction the media is pushing them. Which leads to the next point.

The true nature of this set-up should be clear at a glance. According to the new conventional wisdom, Israel has become tyrannical, forgetting their own experience with the Nazis, and becoming what they once fled. In this narrative, the Palestinian people have been provoked into choosing a leadership that is on the fighting, radical end of things, but this is understandable, root causes, so forth and etc.

But one time, in the middle of one of these brawls, I heard a spokesman for Hamas outlining their demands. And one of the central things they wanted was the border crossings into Israel opened so that inhabitants of Gaza could get into Israel freely.

Huh? How does that fit with the narrative? When Jews escaped from the Nazis, did they form enclaves outside the Nazi borders, demanding to be let back in? No, because the Nazis really were... Nazis. There was genuine tyranny there, not just agitprop tyranny projected for the cameras.

Galatians 6:1 gives us the principle that when you set out to correct others, you should also be ever mindful of your own temptations. This is a principle that

Paul has in mind for life within the body of Christ, but I think it has good applications for situations like this as well. So I don't go into things like this braced to resist the temptations that Hamas faces, or the temptations that Israel faces. I can resist other people's temptations all day long and not even break a sweat. But I am a hardline conservative, and this means that one of the things I should keep a weather eye out for is the tendency of certain kinds of conservatives to get a bad case of the Jew thing. I want to exercise the kind of climate control that prevents antisemitism from taking root and growing anywhere around me.

Now when I am on the look-out for this problem, I am not looking for simple disagreement with Israel, or disagreement with her wars, or objections to Zionism, or disagreement with the dispensational-style support for Israel (which is, as a friend said this morning, a belief that Israel has got to be destroyed in a certain *way*, and so we must defend her until then). The issue is not the position held. I believe that Jews need Christ in order to be forgiven for their sins, and that if they die without Christ, then they die unforgiven. And I am well aware that in some quarters the mere embrace of such positions makes you *de facto* antisemitic. But the fact that I would be falsely charged with antisemitism does not make real antisemitism nonexistent.

Think about it for a minute. It *does* exist, and it exists in *our* circles, and it is as repulsive here as it is

anywhere. The tell-tale sign is not found in mere disagreement with Israeli policy; the tell-tale sign is to
be found in the inability to discuss these things without getting whipped up into a topping suitable for a
meringue pie.

And this leads to my next point. It is an undisputed
fact that Hamas considers itself to be absolutely free
to launch rockets into Israeli population centers—
thousands of rockets over an extended period of time.
Israel says they are doing it, and Hamas says they are
doing it. Nobody that I know of is maintaining that
Hamas is saying, "Rockets? What rockets?"

In the Hamas view of war, such civilians are a
legitimate target. They do not subscribe to just war
theory as it has developed in the West. But Israel *is*
constrained by just war theory, along with the customs of the West.

Now follow this carefully: This does not mean
that Israel in *fact* conducts all her wars in ways that
are in substance just. It does mean she acknowledges
that she is obliged to. This makes both justice and
hypocrisy possible. I am not saying with regard to any
particular military action which one it is. The embrace
of a standard means that it is possible to fall short of
that standard. The standard for war embraced by the
West was violated by our firebombing of Dresden,
for example. That was hypocrisy, sure enough. But if
we accepted that kind of thing as standard operating

procedures, no apologies needed, then it would be far worse. Hamas operates in that "far worse" category, a category of unalloyed cruelty.

So my point does not depend at all on the *actual* righteousness of Israel. If an adversary is launching rockets at your civilians, then you have the right to respond the way Israel has responded in the past—at least, you have the right to do what Israel has in the past *pretended* to do. Either way, from where we sit in the nickel seats, when Hamas provokes a war, Hamas can get one. If Israel is biting and gouging where the ref can't see... well, the ref can't see.

If Israel's civilized "just war" behavior is all a pretense, then *that* is a legitimate subject for discussion, and an investigative reporter should be allowed (at least in our book) to report on it without incurring automatic charges of antisemitism. Of course. But such a reporter should be aware of the fact that he is stepping into a large fever swamp full of antisemitism, and in order to do his job right, he will have to labor mightily to distinguish himself from the surrounding vitriol. If his report begins: "GAZA: This afternoon, guided by Satan, the *Jooos* bombed a day care center..." then I crave your indulgence if I stop reading right there.

If you don't want to be taken for a whackadoodle, then stop writing like a whackadoodle. If you are sober and sane, then don't link to crazed sites. If you are crazed yourself, then don't link to sober and sane sites because chances are a bunch of people will not bother to get past your, um, strangely *focused* introduction to them.

Suppose a bunch of Israeli generals, with a few winks and nods from the government, said to themselves, "Let's kill us a bunch of Palestinian civilians while we're at this. We will call it collateral damage, and tell the weak sisters at the UN that it was a regrettable circumstance of war. But here, at our private cocktail party, we will toast one another on all the women and children we killed on purpose. I mean, absolutely on purpose." Suppose that kind of thing has gone on. That doesn't change the public circumstance. Israel still has the public right to do what they pretend to do. If they are actually doing it, then it is a just response. If they are pretending to do it, then it is unjust—but we, here on the other side of the world, don't know that. If we hate Jews, we might *think* we know it in our hearts, but for all the sensations of assurance that might provide, it is still not the same thing as actual proof.

One of the things a lot of people need to learn how to do is make political determinations, whenever possible, based on the undisputed out-in-the-open facts. This is possible a *lot* more than is pretended otherwise. The alternative is to try to make determinations based on the contested behind-the-scenes-facts, and this is an invitation to spiral into the fascinating worlds of conspiracy-thot.

As noted above, it is simply beside the point to claim that the Israelis do this same kind of thing privately. But if it is private, it isn't the same kind of thing, now is it? Remember that terrorism is a public tactic. It is either not the same kind of thing because it didn't ever happen, or it is not the same kind of thing because the Israelis are not deliberately targeting civilians in such a way as to ensure that the whole stinking world knows about it. In other words, all we have to do is look at the *public* facts in order to determine who is being publicly wicked. And if someone is being publicly wicked, we have no business carrying any water for them.

If Christians over here, purporting to have a biblical worldview, start expressing their sympathy with the *open* skunks because they are convinced that the *hidden* skunks are just as bad, then it does not astonish me at all that people don't want to listen to us.

Israel is a Western nation. We understand her, sins and all, while we have a very dim understanding of the thugocracies that surround her on every side. I am opposed to any solutions that pretend to understand Arab hostility to the Jews in Western terms. Hamas is not the League of Women Voters. *Unlike her enemies,* Israel repudiates the deliberate targeting of civilians as a matter of open policy. Israel's enemies have no problem "taking responsibility for" the bombing of a teenage pizza hang-out *because* it was filled with non-combatants. Those who ignore this reality, and they are legion, have no right to try to bring a biblical perspective to bear on the conflict—because they have no biblical perspective to bring. Those who cannot see the difference between Israel and her enemies on this point are what might be called "blind."

CHAPTER 4
Judaism: Good, Bad, and Ugly

MANY CHRISTIANS NAIVELY BELIEVE that Orthodox Jews are basically on the same page with Christians, only they are running one testament short. This kind of superficial treatment of Judaism and Christianity reduces everything to whether you say "Merry Christmas" or "Happy Hanukkah." Do you put up Christmas lights, or do you light a menorah? Many Christians, particularly some in the dispensational tradition, regard our differences with the Jews as extreme denominational differences, but still somehow within the pale.

But modern Judaism is *not* the religion of the Old Testament. It is something else entirely. It is not the biblical faith with Jesus left out. Imagine a faithful Jew residing in Spain just before the apostle Paul's visit there. What he believes, looking forward to a Messiah to come, and not knowing that He *has* come, is a very different proposition from a twenty-first century Jew, looking forward to a Messiah to come, and vigorously denying that Jesus was that Messiah. The situations are entirely different.

In order to understand this, we have to understand something of what the Talmud is.

TALMUDIC JUDAISM: THE UGLY SIDE

There are two versions of the Talmud—the Babylonian Talmud and the Jerusalem or Palestinian Talmud. The latter is smaller and contains earlier material. The Babylonian Talmud is the one usually referred to as it received better editing, and the subjects it addresses are less parochial or local. The Jerusalem Talmud has not had nearly the same impact as the Babylonian, so for the sake of space we will focus on the latter. The Babylonian Talmud comes in two parts: the *Mishnah* and the *Gemara*. The *Mishnah* is a collection of the oral traditions of the rabbis between 200 BC and AD 200, and the *Gemara* is a collection of commentaries on the *Mishnah* formed over the following three centuries.

When Jerusalem was destroyed in AD 70, the Temple sacrifices were shut down completely—but the entire Mosaic system presupposed the sacrifices of bulls and goats. The Jews who had become Christians were able to fill that Temple vacancy with the once-for-all sacrifice of Christ on the cross. This was the whole point of the book of Hebrews. The Christian church was the Temple of the living God, and so there was no need to struggle with this Temple vacancy. The Messiah had predicted that the Temple was going to be leveled. It was clearly all part of God's plan.

But the Jews who had not believed in Christ needed to "reinvent themselves." They had the same vacancy to deal with, and they needed to fill it with *something*. What they filled it with was the tradition of the elders. This process had begun *before* the Temple was destroyed, and Jesus had actually chided them for it. They were setting aside the Word of God—including what the Word taught about the Temple—and they were replacing it with the traditions of men. When Jesus cleansed the Temple, this was His charge against them. Instead of revering the Temple as a house of prayer, they had transformed it into a den of thieves (Mark 11:17).

Replacing the Temple system with the tradition of the elders resulted in what might be called the triumph of Pharisaism, and the Talmud is the monument to that triumph. Prior to the judgment on Jerusalem, they already had a few centuries of a wrong-footed head start; the traditions that Jesus so violently rejected were the traditions of the first half of the Talmudic stream. Indeed, the Talmudic traditions of the elders were the reason *why* Jerusalem was judged so severely.

Now this Babylonian Talmud is a beast, running to 34 volumes, and they are not slender volumes either. The Talmud was not completed in the time of Christ, but it was complete enough for Jesus to be at war with it. You don't need to drink the whole bottle of vinegar to know that it is vinegar.

So according to Christ, the rabbis had been supplanting the teaching of the Word of God for the sake of their traditions, and they had been doing this for several centuries.

> He answered and said unto them, Well hath Esaias prophesied of you hypocrites, as it is written, This people honoureth me with their lips, but their heart is far from me. Howbeit in vain do they worship me, teaching for doctrines the commandments of men. For laying aside the commandment of God, ye hold the tradition of men ... making the word of God of none effect through your tradition, which ye have delivered: and many such like things do ye. (Mark 7:6–13)

To be clear, what Jesus is talking about here is a gradually forming Talmud.

So Jesus rejected the rabbinic tradition that was developing—and the rabbis also rejected Him. The next several centuries of Talmudic development occurred in the Christian era, and did so in direct opposition to Christ, and to Christians. In the heat of that religious conflict, it is not surprising that the polemical element could get pretty vitriolic. According to the Talmud, Gentiles who opposed the Jews were to spend eternity in boiling hot semen. Christians, together with Jesus, were relegated to an eternity in boiling hot excrement.[1]

It can get pretty weird in other ways also. Rabbi Eleazar taught that "bone of my bone, and flesh of my flesh" in Genesis meant that Adam had sexual intercourse with all of the beasts, but was unsatisfied until he was given Eve.[2] I dare say he was not satisfied.

It was also taught that if a man had sex with a boy under the age of nine, there need be no guilt incurred. Another rabbi said that the age under which there was no guilt was the age of three.[3]

It must be remembered that the Talmud is such a morass of contradictory and confusing doctrines that we should not attribute to every rabbi the specific perversions or oddments of another rabbi. I am not saying that every conservative or Orthodox Jew would agree

1. Gary North, *The Judeo-Christian Tradition* (Tyler, TX: Institute for Christian Economics, 1990), 86.
2. Ibid., 87.
3. Ibid.

with such sentiments, or even that they are aware of their existence. The Talmud is an enormous sprawl of words, formed over the course of centuries. It was assembled by fallen human beings, and so is an amalgam of good sense, exegetical insights, weirdness, and perverseness. Some of the gold, the exegetical insights, will be addressed in the next section.

But all the rabbis, and all the more conservative Jews today who regard the Talmud as representing the traditions of the elders, have to deal with the reality of rank embarrassments. They really are there. And *embarrassments* they are.

Imagine being in possession of all the issues of *Cosmopolitan* magazine, on the assumption that the magazine had had a run of some seven hundred years. You would have quite a range of material—from articles on how to be a dutiful homemaker in the 1890s, to more up-to-date porno articles on 800 ways to drive your man wild in bed. But if you were foolish enough to declare that the entire collection was a compendium of the "teaching of the elders of our people," you would have some exegetical challenges in front of you.

The Talmud is like the Everglades, a vast and tangled swamp. Those grotesque examples just given are specimens of particularly nasty toads or snakes that have been caught in there. And so while we should acknowledge that there are many Jews who would repudiate all such things with disgust, they still want to praise the pristine beauty of the Everglades, and they still want to live near them.

The purpose of this section is to show that Christianity and Judaism are two distinct religions. And the difference is much wider than the fact that Christians have both the Old and New Testaments while the Jews have the Old Testament. Rather, the distinction is that Christians have the entire Word of God while the Jews have an Old Testament which they have in effect nullified with their traditions. This process was already well underway when Jesus rebuked it, and it has continued down to the present, with the Jews unrepentant.

This is done by detailed casuistry, a particular kind of very close reasoning that feels the liberty to disregard the plain teaching of the Scriptures. Talmudic reasoning—and if we wanted to make this sting, we might call it jesuitical reasoning—is a rationalizing and special-pleading attempt to evade the authority of the Word of God.

For example, Leviticus says, "And thou shalt not let any of thy seed pass through the fire to Molech, neither shalt thou profane the name of thy God: I am the LORD" (Lev. 18:21).

In contrast, the *Mishnah* says, "He who gives his seed to Molech incurs no punishment unless he delivers it to Molech and causes it to pass through the fire. If he gave it to Molech but did not cause it to pass through the fire, or the reverse, he incurs no penalty, unless he does both."[4]

The commentary on this in the *Gemara* says, "The Mishnah teaches idolatry and giving to Molech. R. Abin said: Our Mishnah is in accordance with the view that Molech worship is not idolatry... R. Simeon said: If to Molech, he is liable; if to another idol, he is not."[5]

And this: "R. Aha the son of Rabbi said: If one caused all his seed to pass through the fire to Molech, he is exempt from punishment, because it is written, of *thy seed* implying, but not all thy seed."[6]

What do you think Jesus would have said about the rabbinical teaching that to lift and carry a chair on the Sabbath would have been permissible, but to drag it would be to break the Sabbath? This is because lifting is only a minor effort, while dragging a chair might break the surface of the ground. And that would be plowing.

The formation of the Talmud was not completed when the Lord Jesus confronted the rabbis of His day. But it was far enough along for the Lord to object to certain key principles that were taking shape. We will see in the next section that it was not all of that caliber, but enough of it was for the Lord to say that it amounted to a "setting aside" of what God had revealed through Moses.

4. North, *The* Judeo-Christian *Tradition*, 92.
5. Ibid.
6. Ibid.

TWO CHEERS FOR THE TALMUD

Now at this point, you might be forgiven for thinking the Talmud is a gigantic slag heap of worthlessness, and nobody should waste anyone's time trying to sort through it.

If you want to treat the whole thing as a monument that is worthy of the elders, you do in fact have quite a challenge before you. But it is not a slag heap of worthlessness. There is a mountain range here, and while many of the mines are just long, empty tunnels, some with dead rats in them, there are also gold and silver mines that are quite productive.

Jesus did trash the reputation of the Pharisees for us, but He was not entirely dismissive. Matthew 23 is crammed full of fierce denunciations of pietistic and scrupulous folly. However, Jesus begins that chapter with a backhanded compliment: "Then spake Jesus to the multitude, and to his disciples, Saying, The scribes and the Pharisees sit in Moses' seat: All therefore whatsoever they bid you observe, that observe and do; but do not ye after their works: for they say, and do not" (Matt. 23:1–3). The Pharisees, He said, sat in Moses' seat. It would be appropriate to do what they said, but not to imitate them in their actions. Their fundamental problem was their hypocrisy.

And so it has to be said here that Christ was much closer doctrinally to the Pharisees than he was to the Sadducees. And the apostle Paul was trained as a Pharisee under Gamaliel, and even after his conversion was willing still to identify himself in that way: before the Sanhedrin, he cried out that he was a Pharisee, the son of Pharisees, and that he was on trial because of his belief in the resurrection of the dead (Acts 23:6).

The Pharisees were a highly respected group in Israel, at least until Jesus got done with their reputation. It is my opinion (approaching a conviction) that Ezra was the first Pharisee, or at least he began the scribal tradition that became the Pharisees. If we were looking for a term in English that had a similar etymology and cachet as "Pharisee," it would be something like the term "Puritan." Both words indicate some kind of desire for separation and holiness. Like Pharisaism, Puritanism was noble in its founding, had some glorious exemplars, was doctrinally rigorous, went to seed after a few centuries, and is now easy to mock.

At the time of Christ, there were about 6,000 Pharisees in Israel. They were, generally speaking, well-to-do businessmen who had the time and money to devote themselves to a scrupulous pursuit of holiness. This is perhaps what accounted for the disciples' astonishment when Jesus taught how hard it was for rich men to enter the kingdom. "Who then can be saved?" was their reaction (Matt. 19:25). Money meant that you could carve out the time needed for pious pursuits. At least, that is what they could tell themselves. But the Pharisees, we are told, were lovers of money (Luke 16:14). What their "project" consisted of was wanting rank-and-file Israelites to conform to a level of holiness and separation that the Torah required of priests—and that was a standard an ordinary laboring man could not possibly achieve.

The Sadducees only accepted the inspiration of the Pentateuch, and not of the prophets. The Sadducees did not believe in angels and spirits, while the Pharisees did. The Sadducees did not acknowledge a general resurrection of the dead at the end of history, while the Pharisees did. You can see why Jesus could say that they sat in Moses' seat, and that we should listen to them. They were the conservatives, while the Sadducees were the liberals.

But liberals can be honest in their unbelief, and conservatives can be dishonest in their profession of faith. You can believe in the resurrection of the dead, and also devour widows' houses.

So with that setting the stage, what can we say in favor of the Talmud?

One of the things that separates Jews and Christians is that the Christians see the various messianic streams of the Old Testament all coming together in Christ. For Christians, the suffering servant of Isaiah describes the Messiah in one phase of His ministry, while His apocalyptic judgments are fulfilled in another phase by this same Christ. In contrast, the rabbinical tradition has room for multiple Messiahs, which the Jews do not necessarily see as coming together in one person.

One of the treasures of the Talmud is one of these messianic traditions, kept alive by the rabbis over the course of centuries, and virtually unknown to Christians. But once made aware of this tradition, the natural Christian response is to see it fulfilled in Jesus Christ as well. Jews naturally want to keep it distinct, and a number of indicators that point to Jesus of Nazareth are part of the reason why this rabbinical tradition was largely kept hidden from Christian scholars until the nineteenth century.

In short, there are a number of messianic passages that do not appear to apply to Messiah ben David, which is where Christian interpreters (for obvious reasons) tend to concentrate their attention. The Jewish teachers were very aware of these other passages, and interpreted them as applying to a different Messiah, Messiah ben Joseph. They had no expectation at the time that all the messianic promises had to converge in one person, and so they felt free to interact with the implications of those texts within the boundaries of their worldview. They probably did not want to draw the attention of Christian interpreters to the fact that there was a messiah figure in the Old Testament who was going to be the son of *Joseph*.

Before getting to the scriptural argument, I need to point out the larger argument of this section. It is that there is a significant messianic theme running through Scripture that the rabbis were aware of over the course of centuries, but which Christians, reading the same Old Testament, were largely unaware of. The point is not that the rabbis rightly applied it to Jesus, because they obviously did not. The point is that they were close observers of the text, and often saw relevant things there that Christian interpreters did not—but should have.

Now Christians understand that Messiah ben David is of course Jesus Christ. He is from the tribe of Judah, the tribe to which the scepter belonged. But this other Messiah is Messiah ben Joseph. I am just going to state the rudiments of the case here—for the rest I would urge you to consult David Mitchell's book, *Messiah ben Joseph*. As I have told a number of people, there are portions of this book that are good enough to melt your face.

Prophecies that a descendant of Joseph would rule the world are found both in Jacob's blessing, and in the blessing that Moses gave to Joseph. The blessings are astonishing in their breadth and depth, and appear to include worldwide dominion. Jacob says this:

> Joseph is a fruitful bough, even a fruitful bough
> by a well; Whose branches run over the wall ...
> Even by the God of thy father, who shall help
> thee; And by the Almighty, who shall bless thee
> with blessings of heaven above, blessings of the
> deep that lieth under, blessings of the breasts,
> and of the womb: The blessings of thy father have
> prevailed above the blessings of my progenitors

> unto the utmost bound of the everlasting hills:
> They shall be on the head of Joseph, and on the
> crown of the head of him that was separate from
> his brethren. (Gen. 49:22–26)

And Moses does something similar for Joseph:

> And of Joseph he said, Blessed of the LORD be his
> land.... Let the blessing come upon the head of
> Joseph, and upon the top of the head of him that
> was separated from his brethren. His glory is like
> the firstling of his bullock, and his horns are like
> the horns of unicorns: With them he shall push
> the people together to the ends of the earth: And
> they are the ten thousands of Ephraim, and they
> are the thousands of Manasseh. (Deut. 33:13–17)

Now Joseph is one of the standout characters of the
Old Testament and is clearly a type of Christ in many
respects. Rachel was barren and conceived through the
intervention of God (Gen. 30:2), and Mary was a vir-
gin and so conceived miraculously (Matt. 1:18). Joseph
was beloved of his father (Gen. 37:3) as Jesus was by
His (Matt. 3:17; 17:5). Joseph's brothers rejected him
(Gen. 37:8) as did the brothers of Jesus (John 7:5).
Joseph was stripped and mocked (Gen. 37:19, 23), and
Jesus was stripped and mocked (Matt. 27:28). Joseph
was sold for silver (Gen. 37:28) and so was Jesus (Matt.

26:15). Joseph was thirty years old when he began his public ministry in Egypt (Gen. 41:46), and Jesus was around thirty when He began His ministry (Luke 3:23). Joseph is the savior of the world (Gen. 45:7), and Jesus is the Savior of the world (Acts 13:23). There is much more, but this should suffice.

On top of all that, the Old Testament form of the name of Jesus is Joshua. Joshua, the successor of Moses, and the conqueror of Canaan, was an Ephraimite—the son of Joseph. And notice also that Jesus in the New Testament is reckoned as the legal son of a man named Joseph (Luke 3:23). Physically, Jesus was clearly descended from Judah (along with both Joseph and Mary). But typologically He was the heir of the great promises delivered to Ephraim.

What I have mentioned here is just a fraction of the evidence. Mitchell's book is a work of dense scholarship, so you might want to take it slow. But it is rich. And an essential part of the richness is seen in how it displays the meticulous and detailed knowledge of the text of Scripture displayed by the rabbis. It is simply astonishing—astonishing both that they saw so much in the text, and that they missed so much in the fulfillment.

IS JUDEO-CHRISTIANITY A THING?

This book could be regarded as one of my periodic forays into the tangled thicket of "what gives with Israel?"

You are to imagine it as me putting on a gray coat and blue trousers in order to walk between the lined-up armies on the eve of Gettysburg, as my penultimate and earnest plea for peace.

I recently finished reading *The Magna Carta of Humanity* by Os Guinness, a writer I have long appreciated and admired, and around the same time I read *Christian Nationalism* by Andrew Torba (of Gab fame) and Andrew Isker. In many ways these three gents are attacking the same target, that target being the spirit of the revolutionary and progressive left. But there is one area where the divide between them could not be wider, and that divide, as you may have guessed, has to do with Israel.

Guinness argues that we are in a moment of true crisis in the West, which is true enough, and I really like how he frames it as a choice between the spirit of 1776, the way of liberty, and the spirit of 1789, the way of bondage. These dates are, respectively, the dates of the American Revolution and the French Revolution, which he (*rightly*) sees as mortal enemies. They are two different paths to two different places, liberty and totalitarianism respectively, and so they are utterly at odds.

> America cannot endure permanently half 1776 and half 1789. The compromises, contradictions, hypocrisies, inequities, and evils have built up unaddressed. The grapes of wrath have

ripened again, and the choice before America is plain. Either America goes forward best by going back first, or America is about to reap a future in which the worst will once again be the corruption of the best.[7]

Now Guinness traces the genius of the American experiment back to Sinai, where the civic gift of form and freedom together were first manifested to the world. He does this with learning and erudition, and I agree with just about everything he says. But there is still a fly in the ointment. It is a book full of wisdom, but it really strikes me as a Christless wisdom.

The reason for this is that he is heavily dependent on the insights and observations of Rabbi Jonathan Sacks, a distinguished scholar who served as the Chief Rabbi of the United Hebrew Congregations of the Commonwealth, and who was a member of the House of Lords. Sacks, too, has a lot of good things to say, but for obvious reasons, Jesus is not going to be a big part of it.

This leads Guinness to write as though there are *two* true religions, Judaism and Christianity, and with another one, Islam, hovering somewhere in the Abrahamic ballpark. The Jews have Yom Kippur while Christians have the death, burial, and resurrection of

7. Os Guinness, *The Magna Carta of Humanity* (Downers Grove, IL: InterVarsity Press, 2021), 27.

Jesus. This strikes me as theologically incoherent. The interesting thing is that Guinness doesn't make any attempt to resolve the question. He is earnestly seeking to save a Judeo-Christian civilization, and sees no need to defend that construct. He just assumes it.

But if the Jews are right and Jesus did *not* rise from the dead, then we Christians of all men are most to be pitied (1 Cor. 15:19). And if He *did* rise from the dead, then modern Judaism is an attempt to have a Messiah-based religion while leaving the Messiah out of it. But that is like, as the old illustration goes, putting on a production of Hamlet, and leaving out the prince of Denmark.

In the meantime, Torba and Isker have no use for a Judeo-Christian anything, and yet are at war with the same progressive left that Guinness is fighting. Their fourth chapter is entitled "This Is Not a 'Judeo-Christian' Movement," in case you were wondering. Put all this together, and I have myself the framework for a section in this book.

So, despite the fact that it will be a glorious tangle, like three extension cords stiff with cold that we found in the garage, let us dump it all on the table anyhow.

In the Protestant Reformation, with the cry of *ad fontes*, which means "back to the sources," not only were the Reformers the foremost patristic scholars of their day, but they also went back to learn Hebrew from the rabbis. This contributed to a great advance in learning with regard to the Old Testament, but it also caused some dislocations with some unstable souls, who shot off into various forms of anti-Trinitarianism. If you are interested in that subject, you can consult Ben Merkle's dissertation on it, published by Oxford University Press, and heartily commended to you by none other than his father-in-law.[8]

And the same kind of thing happens today. A Christian exegete can profit greatly, *as I have done*, by consulting work done on the Old Testament text by Jewish scholars. Robert Alter comes to mind.

However, as we've already seen, modern rabbinic Judaism is not the religion of the Old Testament. They are not actually following Moses. Jesus taught all Christians that the traditions of the elders had caused the Jewish leaders to "set aside" the requirements of Moses, observing their own ideas instead (Matt. 15:3). And this happened when their traditions had more going for them—they still had the Temple, for example, and the sacrifices that Moses required. But then, after the destruction of the Temple in AD 70, all they had left were their erroneous traditions. This is why modern Judaism is best considered a heresy of the Old Testament faith, and not a representation of it. To be a Christian is to maintain that the fulfillment of the Old

8. Benjamin R. Merkle, *Defending the Trinity in the Reformed Palatinate: The Elohistae* (Oxford: Oxford Theology and Religion Monographs, 2015), 27.

Testament is in the Christ of the New Testament, and not in rabbinic Judaism.

Now, it's important to note that modern Judaism is not one great monolithic thing. Jews are all over the map, from ultra-orthodox Hasidim, including the mysticism of the Kabbalah, to the hard secularists in the Jewish state, to the reasonable conservatives like Prager or Shapiro. Some Jewish groups would be as far away from Christianity as the Sufi Muslims would be, and are kind of out there, while others have inched back toward the Christian center and are just Unitarians with yarmulkes.

To illustrate, and keep things within the sabbatarian world, if I say that Seventh Day Adventism is a heresy, it does not follow that every Adventist is out there doing nefarious things. Some of them can get really legalistic, and some of it can get really weird doctrinally speaking, as happens within Judaism, but a lot of other Adventists just go to med school at Loma Linda, and do a superb job as your family pediatrician, keeping all your kids healthy.

And this is where I want to push back on an element of what I am seeing in the Torba/Isker book. They see, correctly, that Guinness is wrong about modern Judaism as just another form of biblical faith. Talmudic Judaism really was a distortion of God's Word. But you can't really draw a straight line from that to various modern ills like communism, environmentalism, globalism, and the like—historic Judaism and contemporary Judaism are far too variegated to do so.

A PRODIGAL PEOPLE

One final point. The Jews are unbelievers—but they are not "just one more" unbelieving group. To illustrate the point, let me repurpose the parable of the prodigal son. Keep in mind that I am repurposing it, not trying to interpret it.

The Gentiles were the wastrel younger brother, and when we came back to our father, he had the fatted calf killed to throw a feast for us, and he hired a jazz band so there could be some swing dancing. Some might have argued that the younger brother scarcely needed to go to another *party*, but his father thought differently. Now the Jews are the older brother who heard the music and dancing from the driveway, and who therefore refused to come in.

The Jews are our estranged older brother. And this estrangement is *not permanent*. Not only does the father win back his younger son, he also is eventually reconciled to his older son. This is because the "gifts and the calling of God are irrevocable" (Rom. 11:29). The fact that the estrangement is not permanent, contra Torba, does not mean that there is no real estrangement, contra Guinness. The Jews, like every other sinful tribe and nation, must come to Christ.[9] But they will come.

So pray for the conversion of the Jews. The party is now in full swing, and we are enjoying it, but we still keep looking past the curtains, out to the driveway. Dad is still talking to him. When he comes in, the party can really start.

9. It is often said that Ashkenazi Jews are not Jews at all, and that there is not a drop of Abraham's blood in their veins. And so it is maintained that this is all a lot of fuss and bother over a bunch of nothing. "A gift is not irrevocable if it was never given." This overlooks the fact that being a Jew was always about *covenant*, and not about DNA. The first generation of Jews were those of Abraham's house, all the males who were circumcised (Gen. 17:27). Three chapters earlier, when Abraham went to war on behalf of Lot, there were 318 men. I dare say that a number of them did not have any of Abraham's blood in their veins. Ashkenazi and Sephardic Jews are Jews by *covenant*. And because they are Jews by covenant, it will be a piece of cake for God to graft them into the olive tree again. I mean, if He could graft the *Scythians* into the tree in the first place (Col. 3:11), He can graft in anybody—especially the natural branches (Rom. 11:24).

CHAPTER 5

Jews and Judeans

THE CHRISTIAN FAITH IS SOMETIMES accused of antisemitism because the New Testament, and particularly the gospel of John, makes mention of "the Jews," and in contexts where they are represented as the villains. (We have to set aside for a moment the fact that John himself was a Jew, in the sense that he was descended from Abraham.) However, the word *Ioudaios* can be translated either as "Jew" or as "Judean," and this frequently affects how the account is to be read.

If *Ioudaios* is translated as "Jew," this means a Jew is being contrasted with the Gentiles. If it is translated as "Judean," the primary contrast is with the

Galileans—although it could also be in contrast with other groups as well: Samaritans, say. The parallel is not exact, but we do something similar with the word "Yank" or "Yankee." It can mean a New Englander as opposed to other Americans, or it can mean Americans over against the rest of the world.

A simple review of the instances where the term *Ioudaios* is used can show us contextual reasons for taking it in one sense or the other.

For example, the apostle Peter was a fisherman from Galilee, and yet, when he preaches to Cornelius, he introduces himself as a Jew: "And he said unto them, Ye know how that it is an unlawful thing for a man that is a Jew to keep company, or come unto one of another nation; but God hath shewed me that I should not call any man common or unclean" (Acts 10:28).

Paul, who was from the tribe of Benjamin, calls himself a Jew in Acts 21: "But Paul said, I am a man which am a Jew of Tarsus, a city in Cilicia, a citizen of no mean city: and, I beseech thee, suffer me to speak unto the people" (Acts 21:39; cf. 22:3).

Although Benjamin was historically part of the southern kingdom, Paul is not likely calling himself a Judean here because the phrase he uses is "a Jew of Tarsus," a Gentile city.

In another place, he appears to set the contrast plainly as being an order of priority—Jew first, and then Gentiles. This clearly means Jews as opposed to

Gentiles. "For I am not ashamed of the gospel of Christ: for it is the power of God unto salvation to every one that believeth; to the Jew first, and also to the Greek" (Rom. 1:16).

So where might *Ioudaios* mean "Judean"?

The apostle John was a fisherman from Galilee, and so there are places where modern readers might think he was taking a shot at *Jews* when he was actually being critical of *Judeans*. This possibility is perhaps most clear in John 7: "After these things Jesus walked in Galilee: for he would not walk in Jewry, because the Jews sought to kill him" (John 7:1).

If it were just descendents of Abraham who wanted to kill Him, they were certainly plentiful in Galilee as well. But Judeans were not. The word rendered "Jewry" here is *Ioudaia*—Judea. The reason Jesus was spending time in Galilee (where everyone was Jewish in the modern sense, including Jesus) was because He was staying away from the Judeans down in Judea.

Some might object to this because in the next verse, John calls the feast of tabernacles a feast of the Jews: "Now the Jews' feast of tabernacles was at hand" (John 7:2). Jesus and His brothers all wound up going to that feast, even though they were from Nazareth up in Galilee. Wouldn't that make it a festival for all Jews, Galileans included?

Not quite. A big part of the tension between Judea and Galilee was found in the fact that wealth in the north was a function of trade and manufacturing, while wealth in Judea was a function of the Temple and all of its blood-from-a-turnip services. Jerusalem had become a destination point for numerous pilgrims, and because this system had begun to be used in a way to fleece those pilgrims, it would not have taken much for them to start thinking of the festivals as having been taken hostage by the Judeans.

For just one example of such fleecing, tithes and offerings had to be paid with a special Temple shekel. Ordinary profane shekels could not be used—hence the moneychangers in the Temple. But the exchange rate there was worse than the airport in Amsterdam— it was a 2 to 1 ratio. I can easily imagine a Galilean feeling obligated to go to the Feast of Booths, because it was required by the Torah, but also thinking that the unfortunate festival had been kidnapped by Judean pirates.

Later in John 7, when Nicodemus objects to how the Sanhedrin were talking about Jesus, their contempt for Galilee comes out in the open. "They answered and said unto him, Art thou also of Galilee? Search, and look: for out of Galilee ariseth no prophet" (John 7:52).

Galilee was, according to them, a haven for rubes and cornpones. And they said this despite the fact that Isaiah had given a very clear prophecy of a prophet arising from *Galilee*. "Beyond Jordan, in Galilee of the nations. The people that walked in darkness have seen a great light: They that dwell in the land of the shadow of death, upon them hath the light shined" (Isa. 9:1–2; cf. Matt. 4:15–16).

There are a number of places where John gives us a sharp contrast between Judea and Galilee.

> He left Judaea, and departed again into Galilee. (John 4:3).

> Then when he was come into Galilee, the Galilaeans received him, having seen all the things that he did at Jerusalem at the feast: for they also went unto the feast. (John 4:45)

> This is again the second miracle that Jesus did, when he was come out of Judaea into Galilee. (John 4:54)

And shortly before His crucifixion, when Jesus withdrew to Ephraim, a Judean village, this appears to be an instance of Him withdrawing from the power centers of Judea. "Jesus therefore walked no more openly among the Jews; but went thence unto a country near to the wilderness, into a city called Ephraim, and there continued with his disciples" (John 11:54).

When Jesus came into Jerusalem—acclaimed by the crowd as the Son of David (Matt. 21:9)—He immediately went up to the Temple and began flipping over tables. In doing this, He was attacking the very center of the economy of Jerusalem and Judea—and it was not a trivial amount of money. Jesus called the Temple a den of thieves, and one of the things that thieves know how to do is protect their stash. It was as though He walked up to them and reached out to touch their eyeball. They reacted. But it was the power center of Judea they were protecting, not the fishing villages of Galilee. "Now Caiaphas was he, which gave counsel to the Jews, that it was expedient that one man should die for the people" (John 18:14). This is right at the end of the gospel of John, but the same thing is seen in the first chapter. "And this is the record of John, when the Jews sent priests and Levites from Jerusalem to ask him, Who art thou?" (John 1:19). Notice that "the Jews" sent priests and Levites to Him from *Jerusalem*. That is where the conflict was, that is where the show-down happened.

It is not as though there were no Judeans who believed in Christ. Of course there were; the Triumphal Entry was heralded overwhelmingly by Judeans. And Joseph of Arimathaea—a city in Judea—was the one who saw to it that Jesus received an honorable burial. But notice how his hometown is described by Luke: "(The same had not consented to the counsel and deed of them;) he was of Arimathaea, a city of the Jews: who also himself waited for the kingdom of God" (Luke 23:51).

What does it all mean? When moderns read the New Testament there is sometimes a temptation to read certain references anachronistically. It is not possible to read the gospel of John without concluding "the Jews" are the bad guys. And they certainly were the bad guys, but an anachronistic reading assumes that John meant by "the Jews" the same thing that a modern antisemite means. And this is a basic mistake.

CHAPTER 6

Pharaohs and Herods

ONE OF THE LESSER-KNOWN DOCTRI-
nal themes in Scripture is the idea of ethical reversals.
Sometimes the reversals are connected to classes of
people, and other times to ethnic groups or nations.

Whenever God delivers a group of people, there is
what we might call a temptation cycle, one that we see
operating all through the Scriptures. The cycle goes
like this. God delivers a people from the evil they are
going through. They initially rejoice and express their
gratitude. Then they start to take their new status for
granted. And finally, they become ungrateful, and run
a great risk of becoming the kind of people they were
initially delivered from.

The Christ, when He came, was going to be disruptive in a way that started one of these cycles.

> He hath shewed strength with his arm; He hath scattered the proud in the imagination of their hearts. He hath put down the mighty from their seats, and exalted them of low degree. (Luke 1:51–52).

> And Simeon blessed them, and said unto Mary his mother, Behold, this child is set for the fall and rising again of many in Israel; and for a sign which shall be spoken against. (Luke 2:34)

Now when we are talking about the wealthy and the poor, we can surmise that these reversals are running in the background all the time. In other words, when the mighty are pulled down from their seats, in about five generations, they could easily be the downtrodden of the earth. For all we know, the homeless bum with his "Please help" scrawled on a piece of cardboard is a direct lineal descendant of Napoleon Bonaparte.

It goes the other direction also. When those of low degree are exalted, they need to be reminded pretty regularly that while they might be a princess *now*, their great, great, great grandmother was a charwoman.

But the thing that really throws people off is the enduring presence of ethnic or national markers.

What do I mean? The homeless guy descended from Napoleon has no external indicators that this is so. He has no papers. But this is not the case with a people like the Jews. They know who they are, which is one of the central reasons why they do not know who they are.

This is how John the Revelator made the point. "And their dead bodies shall lie in the street of the great city, which spiritually is called Sodom and Egypt, where also our Lord was crucified" (Rev. 11:8).

The Lord was crucified, of course, in Jerusalem, and John calls them "the great city," but also under the typological names of *Sodom* and *Egypt*. That's a reversal right there. Peter's cryptic remark about the church in Babylon (1 Pet. 5:13) is a likely reference to Jerusalem, another reversal.

We see this done any number of times. Herod the Great was an Idumean, which is another way of saying that he was an Edomite. At the same time, he very much wanted to be accepted as a king of the *Jews*—which is why he went to such great lengths to build such a magnificent Temple. But when the wise men arrived in Jerusalem with their query, Herod determined to kill the hope of Israel; and when the wise men were warned and went home another way, Herod became furious, and ordered all the boys two and under in the region of Bethlehem to be slaughtered. In other words, the king of the Jews had become just like the Pharaoh of Egypt. He also had ordered the execution of little Jewish boys (Exod. 1:22).

Matthew underscores this point when he tells us about the flight into Egypt. "When he arose, he took the young child and his mother by night, and departed into Egypt: And was there until the death of Herod: that it might be fulfilled which was spoken of the Lord by the prophet, saying, Out of Egypt have I called my son" (Matt. 2:14–15).

The prophecy of Hosea (Hos. 11:1) was thus fulfilled in *two* senses. One was literal—the Messiah, as a young child, came up out of the literal nation of Egypt. Just as the old Israel had come up out of Egypt, so also the new Israel, the Lord Jesus, came up out of Egypt. But there was yet another sense in which the prophecy was fulfilled. Israel had become a new Egypt, ruled over by a harsh Pharaoh—Herod. Israel was no longer a safe place for an Israelite boy to be, so God called Him up out of the land of "Egypt." He fled from Egypt to the safety of… Egypt.

In another place, Paul argues that the physical descendants of Sarah the free wife were actually the spiritual descendants of Hagar, the slave concubine. "Which things are an allegory: for these are the two covenants; the one from the mount Sinai, which gendereth to bondage, which is Agar. For this Agar is mount Sinai in Arabia, and answereth to Jerusalem which now is, and is in bondage with her children" (Gal. 4:24–25).

He also (quite insultingly) says that those who prided themselves on their spiritual legacy of circumcision, one that went all the way back to Abraham, were actually just dogs. Not only animals and not men, but unclean animals to boot. "Beware of dogs, beware of evil workers, beware of the concision. For we are the circumcision, which worship God in the spirit, and rejoice in Christ Jesus, and have no confidence in the flesh" (Phil. 3:2–3).

This is at the center of his argument in Romans also. You puff yourself up as a descendent of Abraham—oh, like Ishmael (Rom. 9:7)? Well then, why not puff yourself up as descended from Isaac? Oh, like Esau (Rom. 9:12–13)?

> What if God, willing to shew his wrath, and to make his power known, endured with much long-suffering the vessels of wrath fitted to destruction: And that he might make known the riches of his glory on the vessels of mercy, which he had afore prepared unto glory, Even us, whom he hath called, not of the Jews only, but also of the Gentiles? As he saith also in Osee, I will call them my people, which were not my people; and her beloved, which was not beloved. And it shall come to pass, that in the place where it was said unto them, Ye are not my people; there shall they be called the children of the living God. (Rom. 9:22–26)

God can make sons of Abraham out of rocks, as John the Baptist put it. He can even make sons of Abraham out of Gentiles. "For ye are all the children of God by faith in Christ Jesus. For as many of you as have been baptized into Christ have put on Christ. There is neither Jew nor Greek, there is neither bond nor free, there is neither male nor female: for ye are all one in Christ Jesus. And if ye be Christ's, then are ye Abraham's seed, and heirs according to the promise" (Gal. 3:26-29).

In the flesh, we don't think this way. We want the Jews to stay put. We want the Edomites to remain Edomites. We want the Scythians to continue on as Scythians. That way, when the ethnic groups stay put, our ethnic animosities can also remain secure and predictable. We want Haman the Jew-hater to stay that way (Est. 3:5-6), so he can be the perpetual anti-semitic bad guy. But a few centuries later, we find that some Haman-type is the one who gave Saul of Tarsus the documents he needed to persecute the Christians at Damascus (Acts 9:1-2). As Dostoevsky knew so well, the hard hand of Caiaphas and the hard hand of the Grand Inquisitor could both fit the same glove. *Knowing this is right at the heart of spiritual wisdom.*

Now how and why does all this matter in a discussion of antisemitism? In the long and sorry history of Jewish-Christian relations there have been many dirty deeds. In certain eras, the Jews were the persecutors, not the persecuted. In other eras, it went the other way—largely because the Christians ignored the apostle Paul's warning about this very thing.

If you meet a Jew who will not admit that the Jews of the first century were filled with a hot, persecuting zeal, and were the worst of the worst, then you are talking with someone who is refusing spiritual wisdom. And if you meet a Christian who is unwilling to admit that the pogrom at York in AD 1190 was a Godforsaken hot mess, then you are talking with someone who is also failing at life.

> For ye, brethren, became followers of the churches of God which in Judaea are in Christ Jesus: for ye also have suffered like things of your own countrymen, even as they have of the Jews: Who both killed the Lord Jesus, and their own prophets, and have persecuted us; and they please not God, and are contrary to all men: Forbidding us to speak to the Gentiles that they might be saved, to fill up their sins alway: for the wrath is come upon them to the uttermost. (1 Thess. 2:14–16)

Paul here says that the Christians in Thessalonica suffered at the hands of their own countrymen, and that this happened in just the same way that the churches of God in Judea were attacked by the Judeans. (This, incidentally, is one of the places where I think it is important to render the word *Judaios* as "Judean," and not as "Jew.")

These Judeans killed the Lord Jesus, they killed their own prophets, and they persecuted Paul and his band. They are hostile to "all men," and when it comes to the salvation offered to the Gentiles, they wanted to play the role of the dog in the manger.

They had made many attempts on Paul's life, and they were pretty eager to get it done.

> And there came thither certain Jews from Antioch and Iconium, who persuaded the people, and, having stoned Paul, drew him out of the city, supposing he had been dead. (Acts 14:19)

> And when it was day, certain of the Jews banded together, and bound themselves under a curse, saying that they would neither eat nor drink till they had killed Paul. (Acts 23:12)

But here we come to the cash payout. The New Testament warning, delivered to the Gentiles, is not to become like your persecutors. Do not turn into your adversary. If you turn into what you hate, it indicates you only thought you hated their sleek arrogance of power. You didn't hate it—you envied it.

When God pulls down the persecutors from their seats, and replaces them with the lowly of heart, one of the things that the lowly of heart need to be reminded of is that lowliness of heart does not maintain itself. Over time, it turns into something else.

There are two major places in Paul's writing where he warns the Gentiles not to be caught flat-footed by this principle of reversal. *Antisemitism is a stubborn refusal to heed Paul's warning.*

At Corinth, the Christians were putting on airs because they, unlike the Jews, had some glorious spiritual privileges. And Paul's response is, "So?" You were baptized? So were they (1 Cor. 10:2). Do you have the bread of the Supper? Well, they had spiritual food as well (1 Cor. 10:3). And do you drink the wine of the new covenant? They drank from the Rock that accompanied them, and that Rock was Christ (1 Cor. 10:4). And then Paul gets to his warning. The Jews had everything the Corinthians had, and yet "with many of them God was not well pleased: for they were overthrown in the wilderness" (1 Cor. 10:5). Mark it well, Corinthians. They had what you had, and yet their bodies were scattered all over the wilderness (Heb. 3:17). "Now these things were our examples, to the intent we should not lust after evil things, as they also lusted. . . . Now all these things happened unto them for ensamples: and they are written for our admonition, upon whom the ends of the world are come" (1 Cor. 10:6, 11).

Paul hammers this point home in Romans 11 as well. He made it clear in Romans 8 that no one can lay a charge against God's elect because it is God who justifies (Rom. 8:33). At the same time, he solemnly warns the Roman Christians to not make the same mistake that the unbelieving Jews had done.

> And if some of the branches be broken off, and thou, being a wild olive tree, wert graffed in among them, and with them partakest of the root and fatness of the olive tree; Boast not against the branches. But if thou boast, thou bearest not the root, but the root thee. Thou wilt say then, The branches were broken off, that I might be graffed in. Well; because of unbelief they were broken off, and thou standest by faith. Be not highminded, but fear: For if God spared not the natural branches, take heed lest he also spare not thee. (Rom. 11:17–21)

These natural branches, these unbelieving natural branches, *were by nature persecuting branches*. And if there is one thing that persecutors are, it is highminded. Paul tells the Roman Christians to resist, as a profound temptation, the snare of all such haughty high-mindedness.

And so here is the heart of the matter. What matters is spiritual kinship. Children of the flesh persecute. Children of the promise are the persecuted. This is *the* tell. It is a perennial reality, true in all ages. "Now we,

brethren, as Isaac was, are the children of promise.
But as then he that was born after the flesh persecuted
him that was born after the Spirit, even so it is now"
(Gal. 4:28-29).

And this is why we have the liberty to lump a certain kind of person together with others of a similar
nature. Generalizations are sometimes helpful. But
it is not the color of their flesh that unites them, but
rather the fact of their flesh—the *sarx* as sin principle. They are carnal, of the flesh, worldly. They are of
their father the devil. And the number that belongs
in this category is too great to itemize, although we
can mention a few—Caiaphas and his crew, Tomás de
Torquemada, Saul before his conversion, Bloody Mary,
numerous medieval managers of pogroms, Himmler
as the architect of the Final Solution, the incipient
totalitarianism of Herbert Marcuse and his doctrine
of repressive tolerance, and of course, Stalin. There is
a long chain of other names, but to mention them all
would soon become morbid.

What counts in Scripture is the spiritual family
resemblance. Those who are descended from their
father Abraham look like him. "They answered and
said unto him, Abraham is our father. Jesus saith unto
them, If ye were Abraham's children, ye would do the
works of Abraham" (John 8:39).

And the same principle applies in the opposite
direction. "Ye are of your father the devil, and the lusts

of your father ye will do. He was a murderer from the beginning, and abode not in the truth, because there is no truth in him. When he speaketh a lie, he speaketh of his own: for he is a liar, and the father of it" (John 8:44).

A Pharaoh is as Pharaoh does. A Herod is as Herod does.

CHAPTER 7

The Christ of the Jews for the Gentiles

THE GENTILE WORLD MISSION, OF which Paul was the most notable representative and emissary, was not the point at which God changed His mind about the Jews. Rather, the Gentile world mission was the point at which God fulfilled one of His great promises to the Jews, and at which point the Jewish leaders changed their mind about Jehovah. That particular apostasy is one that we need to understand a bit better than we do. To get this, let's consider a few things from Psalm 117.

The Hallel psalms are psalms of praise—they are Hallelujah psalms, and Psalm 117 concludes with that exclamation of praise. This is a very brief psalm, but although it is brief, it packs a throw weight that is considerable. It is a psalm of praise that encompasses the entire world.

> O praise the LORD, all ye nations: Praise him,
> all ye people. For his merciful kindness is great
> toward us: And the truth of the LORD endureth
> for ever. Praise ye the LORD. (Ps. 117)

The psalm begins with an invitation to "all nations" to render praise to Yahweh, to join together with the Jews in saying *hallelujah* (v. 1). Praise Him, all you *goyim*. Praise Him, all of you tribes (v. 1). And why should we do this? We should do it because His merciful kindness (*hesed*) is great toward us. We should do it because the truth (*emeth*) of Yahweh endures forever (v. 2). This is why we must sing *hallelujah*. So always remember that the salvation of the world is driven by *truth*, and not by lies or flattery.

The apostle Paul defends his mission to the Gentiles in Romans 15, and in the course of that defense, he quotes our passage from Psalm 117. Let's see how he uses it.

> Now I say that Jesus Christ was a minister of the
> circumcision for the truth of God, to confirm
> the promises made unto the fathers: And that

the Gentiles might glorify God for his mercy; as it is written, For this cause I will confess to thee among the Gentiles, and sing unto thy name. And again he saith, Rejoice, ye Gentiles, with his people. And again, Praise the Lord, all ye Gentiles; and laud him, all ye people. And again, Esaias saith, There shall be a root of Jesse, and he that shall rise to reign over the Gentiles; in him shall the Gentiles trust. Now the God of hope fill you with all joy and peace in believing, that ye may abound in hope, through the power of the Holy Ghost. (Rom. 15:8-13)

Christ was made a *deacon* of the circumcision, a servant or a minister of the circumcision. He was born into the tribe of Judah, as a fulfillment of the promise made to David. He was a minister of the Jews. And Paul says here that Christ was made a deacon in this way in order to *confirm* the promises made to the fathers (v. 8). Everything that follows supports that, and everything that follows is also about the gathering in of the Gentiles.

We must piece this together. This is not an exhortation to the Gentiles to praise the Lord when the writer doesn't believe they could ever do anything of the kind. No, we have a prediction that the Gentiles will in fact glorify God for His mercy (v. 9; see 2 Sam. 22:50; Ps. 18:49). In the next verse (v. 10), we have a command that was issued to the Gentiles in Deuteronomy (Deut. 32:43). We see the same thing again in Paul's citation of Psalm 117 (v. 11; Ps. 117:1). And then Paul quotes Isaiah's prophecy that the root of Jesse will in fact spring up, that He will rule over the nations, and that the Gentiles will hope in Him (v. 12; Isa. 11:10). They shall not hurt or destroy in all the holy mountain, and the earth will be as full of the knowledge of the Lord as the waters cover the sea (Isa. 11:9). This is something that is going to happen. It is not something that God just wishes would happen.

So in this context, Paul declares a benediction over the Roman Christians, largely Gentiles, that the God of hope might fill them with joy in believing all of these things, and that they might abound in hope, as the power of the Holy Spirit works in them.

In order to make good sense of this, we have to understand that the Gentiles were *not* the non-Christians of the Old Testament. And in order to do that, we have to distinguish the universalization of the *priesthood* in the New Testament (which actually happened) from the universalization of possible *salvation* (which is not what happened).

We know from the New Testament that Christ is the only way of salvation. "Neither is there salvation in any other: for there is none other name under heaven given among men, whereby we must be saved" (Acts 4:12).

And so, as the Westminster Confession ably puts it, outside the Church there is no ordinary possibility of salvation.

But if we assume that the Jews were the Christians of the Old Testament, this creates enormous problems for us. In the Old Testament, salvation was not limited to just one nation. Rather, the *priesthood* was limited to just one nation. "And ye shall be unto me *a kingdom of priests*, and an holy nation. These are the words which thou shalt speak unto the children of Israel" (Exod. 19:6).

The nation of Israel had priests within their midst, but they were also a nation of priests for the non-Jewish world. So we can say that salvation is *from* the Jews (John 4:22, ESV), but far too many Gentiles are saved in the Old Testament to simply equate "Gentile" with "unbeliever."

Melchizedek was not a Jew, but he was a priest of the Most High God, and the father of all the Jews paid the tithe to him (Gen. 14:18). Jethro, priest of Midian (Exod. 3:1), the father-in-law of Moses, was not a Jew, and yet was a worshiper of the true God. When Ezekiel named three of the godliest men he could think of, two of the three were Gentiles (Ezek. 14:14): Noah lived before there were any Jews, and Job was an Edomite (1 Chron. 1:43). Naaman the Syrian became a worshiper of the true God, and the prophet gave him express standing permission to continue to push his master's wheelchair into the

House of Rimmon (2 Kings 5:18). And let us not forget the massive revival in Nineveh that was brought about through the preaching of Jonah (Matt. 12:41).

When Solomon built the Temple, the structure included a way for Gentiles, pagans, to pray to the true and living God—*while remaining Gentiles*. The language is quite striking.

> Moreover concerning the stranger, *which is not of thy people Israel*, but is come from a far country for thy great name's sake, and thy mighty hand, and thy stretched out arm; if they come and pray in this house; *Then hear thou from the heavens, even from thy dwelling place, and do according to all that the stranger calleth to thee for*; that all people of the earth may know thy name, and fear thee, as doth thy people Israel, and may know that this house which I have built is called by thy name. (2 Chron. 6:32–33)

At the birth of Christ, He was famously visited by magi from the East. These were wise men, most likely Zoroastrian astrologers. They had seen a star in the east and on the basis of that had come to honor the one born king of the Jews. As it is unlikely they got that amount of information from the night sky, I think they were (at least in part) going off the prophecy that Balaam the prophet had made. Remember that

Balaam was a genuine prophet, with a true gift, even though he was a false man (Num. 22:9). And he was a Gentile also, and from the same neck of the woods that the magi were. What had he predicted? "I shall see him, but not now: I shall behold him, but not nigh: *There shall come a Star out of Jacob*, and a Sceptre shall rise out of Israel, and shall smite the corners of Moab, And destroy all the children of Sheth" (Num. 24:17). So a Gentile prophet motivated the Gentile magi to travel an enormous distance in order to worship the Messiah of the Jews.

Paul offers a very interesting argument in Romans 4. He points out that Abraham was justified by faith years before he was circumcised, meaning that he walked by faith as an uncircumcised Gentile for those years, and then after he was circumcised, his faith meant that he was going to be father of the Jews.

> How was it then reckoned? when he was in circumcision, or in uncircumcision? Not in circumcision, but in uncircumcision. And he received the sign of circumcision, a seal of the righteousness of the faith which he had yet being uncircumcised: that he might be the father of all them that believe, though they be not circumcised; that righteousness might be imputed unto them also: And the father of circumcision to them who are not of the circumcision only, but who also walk in the steps

of that faith of our father Abraham, which he had
being yet uncircumcised. (Rom. 4:10–12)

In other words, Abraham is the father of all believing Gentiles.

Finally, when Jesus cleanses the Temple, He drives out the merchants and money changers *from the Court of the Gentiles*. The Gentiles had a court at the Temple, designated for them to worship the true God, and all without becoming Jews first. The clean sacrificial animals represented the Jews, and they had filled up the place that had been reserved for the Gentiles. This is why Jesus' rebuke was a two-edged rebuke. They had filled the Temple with their thievery, and they had excluded the Gentiles by means of it. "And he taught, saying unto them, Is it not written, My house shall be called *of all nations* the house of prayer? but ye have made it a den of thieves" (Mark 11:17).

So the time of the new covenant is a time when salvation explodes into the world, but this is not something that erases a former boundary. Gentiles can be saved now, but they could always be saved. The new glory is that Gentiles can be priests and Levites.

And I will set a sign among them, and I will
send those that escape of them unto the nations,
to Tarshish, Pul, and Lud, that draw the bow, to
Tubal, and Javan, to the isles afar off, that have not

heard my fame, neither have seen my glory; and
they shall declare my glory among the Gentiles.
And they shall bring all your brethren for an offering unto the LORD out of all nations upon horses,
and in chariots, and in litters, and upon mules,
and upon swift beasts, to my holy mountain
Jerusalem, saith the LORD, as the children of Israel
bring an offering in a clean vessel into the house of
the LORD. And I will also take of them for priests
and for Levites, saith the LORD. (Isa. 66:19–21)

Isaiah not only says that Gentiles will hear the
glory of the Lord declared to them. He also says that
priests and Levites will be taken from the ranks of the
Gentiles, which represents a significant change. The
priestly nation has been universalized, and that is why
the basic division now is between Christian and unbeliever. In the New Covenant, God has redrawn the
lines, but not in the way many assume.

All authority, whether in heaven or on earth, has been
given to the Lord Jesus Christ. All the nations belong to
Him, because He bought them with His blood. And this
is the sure foundation of God's good news for this sorry
planet. But what role did the Jews play in setting the
stage for this? If the plan was to go after all the nations,
all the Gentiles, then why a chosen nation at all?

Again, it is not the case that the Old Testament
was for Jews, and then God decided to be a little more

expansive in the New Testament, letting everybody come worship Him now. There *were* changes in the New Testament, but that was not the nature of them. What changed was the potency of the international invitation, not the reality of it.

The Jews were the chosen nation, not in the sense of election to Heaven, but in the sense of a chosen pupil, selected to come to the front to show the rest of the class how the problem was to be solved. When that student does well, he is blessed. He is the class hero. When he messes up, he messes up in front of everybody. But the whole class is always involved. Remember Melchizedek, and Jethro, and Namaan, and the residents of Nineveh, and all the Gentiles who were invited to the court of the Gentiles in the Temple.

Over the centuries, the Jews had been praising Yahweh, praising Jehovah, the covenant God of Israel. Christ came as a minister of the circumcision in order to confirm His promises to them—not to abrogate them, but rather to confirm them. When He came— lived His life as a perfect Jew, was crucified, was buried, and raised again—this was a confirmation that He was in fact the Son of God (Rom. 1:4). As a result of all this, the fundamental Christian confession is that Jesus *is* Yahweh. This means that He is the covenant Lord of *Israel*. "And it shall come to pass, that whosoever shall call on the name of the LORD shall be delivered" (Joel 2:32). Paul quotes this in Romans 10:13, using the

Greek word *kurios* for Yahweh. And just a moment before, Paul told us that the fundamental confession was that "*Jesus* is Lord (*kurios*)."

Never forget that because this priesthood is universal, it must of necessity include ethnic Israel. Their disobedience is only temporary, and they *will* be brought back in again (Rom. 11:23). Antisemitism is about the most anti-gospel frame of mind that can be imagined. And among professed worshipers of Jesus ben David, it is also the silliest. Christ is the Lord of Israel, and this is why He is the Lord of the new Israel as well.

So Gentiles in the Old Testament were not synonymous with unbelievers in the New. Most of them were unbelievers, but it was also possible to be a Gentile and a devout follower of Yahweh.

In the fourth chapter of Acts, the apostles did a great miracle and were challenged on it. By what power or *name* have you done this (Acts 4:7)? They responded that this man stands before you whole by the *name* of Jesus Christ of Nazareth (Acts 4:10). And this led to the great confession: "Neither is there salvation in any other: for there is none other name under heaven given among men, whereby we must be saved" (Acts 4:12).

The necessity of preaching the gospel to every creature today can be seen in this. Nonbelievers are not brought to salvation through the power of an anonymous Christ, working behind the scenes. They are saved through the preaching of the *name*. And if they want to be saved, they must themselves call upon the name. The priesthood of believers has now been expanded to all the nations of men, which is why all men are summoned to believe and be baptized. "And such were some of you: but ye are washed, but ye are sanctified, but ye are justified *in the name of the Lord Jesus*, and by the Spirit of our God" (1 Cor. 6:11). In short, nonbelievers who want to be saved today have an obligation today to repent and believe, calling upon the name of Jesus. Non-Christians have a moral obligation to become Christians.

But in the Old Testament, Gentiles were under no obligation whatsoever to become Jews. They could be saved without becoming Jews, and many of them were saved without becoming Jews. The Jews were not the believers of the Old Testament, but were rather the priestly people of the Old Testament. And they served in this function *for the sake of* the Gentiles nations.

The Jews in the Old Testament era were a priestly nation. But if Gentiles believed in Jehovah, there was certainly a place for them—a place for them *as Gentiles*.

THE TABERNACLE OF DAVID
The apostle Paul tells us, flat out, that the inclusion of the Gentiles together with the Jews was a "great mystery" (Eph. 3:6). It is now plainly revealed in the

new covenant, but after the fact, as we search the Old Testament Scriptures, we can see it everywhere. The establishment and founding of Israel was in fact the hope of the entire world.

One of the surprises in the New Testament is the climax of the Council of Jerusalem. The single biggest controversy in the New Testament church was over whether a person could become a Christian without becoming a Jew first, and so the first great ecumenical council was held to respond to the question. Arguments were presented, and the debate was vigorous. And then, as the proceedings were coming to a head, James, who was presiding at the council, appealed to a passage from Amos: "In that day will I raise up the tabernacle of David that is fallen, and close up the breaches thereof; And I will raise up his ruins, and I will build it as in the days of old" (Amos 9:11).

The passage is an obscure one, at least to us. But James tells us plainly that the reference to the tabernacle of David in Amos meant that the Gentiles as Gentiles were to be included in the Christian church. "Simeon hath declared how God at the first did visit the Gentiles, to take out of them a people for his name. And to this agree the words of the prophets; as it is written, After this I will return, and will build again the tabernacle of David, which is fallen down; and I will build again the ruins thereof, and I will set it up" (Acts 15:16).

That is what David's tabernacle signified.

The building of the first Tabernacle by David was geared to the Gentiles—consider, for example, the role of Obed-edom. And consider also the fact that while the Tabernacle was dedicated with blood sacrifices, it was not *for* blood sacrifices. The Tabernacle (located on Mount Zion) was reserved for music. The Tabernacle of David was therefore a precursor to the international catholicity of the church.

Again, the work of God in the world has always been about the salvation of the nations. So wherever you are in the world, in whatever nation, reading this book, it is two thousand years after the Lord Jesus accomplished your salvation, and three thousand years after King David prophetically enacted it through the sacrifice of his praise.

> For the kingdom is the LORD's: And he is the *governor among the nations*. (Ps. 22:28)

> O *let the nations be glad* and sing for joy: For thou shalt judge the people righteously, and *govern the nations* upon earth. (Ps. 67:4)

> Yea, all kings shall fall down before him: *All nations shall serve him.* (Ps. 72:11)

> *All nations* whom thou hast made *shall come and worship before thee*, O Lord; and shall glorify thy name. (Ps. 86:9)

In order to get a little deeper into all of this, I want to offer a particular reading of Psalm 132. The overall tone of this psalm is unambiguously jubilant, but a number of the details are nevertheless ambiguous. This is said because my reconstruction of the players involved is certainly not the only possible one, but I do think it is reasonable.

This is another song of ascents, given for pilgrims approaching the Temple. We are not told who the author is, but given the subject matter, a reasonable assumption would be that it was written by Solomon. The plea to Jehovah is that He would remember David, and all his afflictions (v. 1). The affliction was related to David's declared intention to fulfill his vow to build a dwelling place for the "Mighty One of Jacob" (vv. 2–5). David had heard of the ark of the covenant while growing up at Ephrathah (or Bethlehem), and how it was located in the fields of Jaar—and he had an intense desire to worship at His footstool (vv. 6–7). This footstool was the ark, which had been at Kiriath-jearim for twenty years prior to the great repentance under Samuel (1 Sam. 7:2), and then stayed in Kiriath-jearim for some more years after that, and then stayed briefly for a few months at the house of Obed-edom (2 Sam. 6:10–11).

The stint at Obed-edom's house was right after the abortive attempt to bring the ark back to Jerusalem. David and Solomon both wanted the ark of God's strength to come into a place of "rest." David brought it to the tabernacle of David located on Zion (2 Chron. 1:4), and then Solomon later brought it up into the Temple on Moriah (1 Kings 8:1).

In both cases, it was a matter of righteous jubilation (v. 9). Solomon links his placement of the ark to the promise made to his father, David (v. 10). Solomon is aware of the fact that God had made an astounding promise to David concerning the future of his dynasty (vv. 11–12; 2 Sam. 7), which He gave right after He sent word through Nathan that David would be denied the privilege of building the Temple. Although David was not permitted to build the Temple, his son honored him when he moved the ark of the covenant to its permanent home.

Solomon goes on. The Lord has chosen Zion as His resting place forever (vv. 13–14). From that place in Zion, Jehovah would bless the poor with bread (v. 15), the priests with salvation (v. 16), the saints with shouts of joy (v. 16). The horn (of authority) will sprout for David (v. 17), such that his enemies will be humiliated, and his crown will shine (v. 18).

And this brings us to the sure mercies of David. David was a dazzling figure in the history of Israel, but we make a great mistake if we overlook how important he was to the *Gentiles*, how fascinating he was to them. His adultery with Bathsheba, and his murder of Uriah, were the two great twin sins of his life, but one of the things that made the murder of Uriah so grotesque was the fact that Uriah was a *Hittite*, doggedly loyal to David. Even when David got him drunk to help cover up his sin, Uriah stayed true to the cause—and in that moment, better to be Uriah drunk than David sober.

But David rubbed shoulders with Gentiles easily (1 Sam. 27:6). He commanded their respect. Consider the behavior of Ittai the Gittite, a man from *Gath* (2 Sam. 15:18)—that was Goliath's hometown—who showed up to serve David on the very eve of Absalom's rebellion, and who then willingly went into exile with him (2 Sam. 15:21).

And when David attempted to bring the ark up from Kiriath-jearim on a cart, and God struck down Uzzah when he touched it, David stored the ark at the house of Obed-edom, another Gittite. I mean, Obed-edom probably graduated from the same high school that Goliath graduated from. What's more, when the ark was finally safe in the tabernacle at Zion, Obed-edom became one of the *porters* there (1 Chron. 16:38).

At the dedication of the Temple, Solomon prayed that God would remember "the mercies of David" (2 Chron. 6:42). And what did Jesus receive upon His resurrection from the dead? He received the sure mercies of David (Acts 13:34), applying to Jesus the promise of Isaiah 55:3.

This all means that we believers, Jew and Gentile together, are the tabernacle of David.

This tabernacle of David on Zion was dedicated with sacrifices (2 Sam. 6:17), but it was not a place constructed for the offering up of blood sacrifices. Rather, it was a tabernacle of music. David was a great musician, and it is not surprising that he built a place for the sacrifices of *praise* (Heb. 13:15). "And they ministered before the dwelling place of the tabernacle of the congregation with singing, until Solomon had built the house of the LORD in Jerusalem: and then they waited on their office according to their order" (1 Chron. 6:32).

These were musical priests, not blood priests. And this is why when Christian congregations gather weekly in order to offer up the sacrifices of praise to God, they ought to be singing a lot. We are the restoration of that tabernacle of music, and it ought to sound like it. Because of the great Son of David, we are all sons and daughters of David. "And in mercy shall the throne be established: And he shall sit upon it in truth in the tabernacle of David, judging, and seeking judgment, and hasting righteousness" (Isa. 16:5).

And all of this should be woven into our understanding of what actually happened on Pentecost. This includes taking note of where it happened... and where it did not.

> And when the day of Pentecost was fully come, they were all with one accord in one place. And suddenly there came a sound from heaven as of

a rushing mighty wind, and it filled all the house where they were sitting. And there appeared unto them cloven tongues like as of fire, and it sat upon each of them. And they were all filled with the Holy Ghost, and began to speak with other tongues, as the Spirit gave them utterance. And there were dwelling at Jerusalem Jews, devout men, out of every nation under heaven. Now when this was noised abroad, the multitude came together, and were confounded, because that every man heard them speak in his own language. (Acts 2:1–6)

Jesus, crucified and risen, ascended into Heaven to be seated at the right hand of the Father. From that exalted place, He had promised to give gifts to men, a promise that was fulfilled in the Church on the day of Pentecost. We of course rejoice that it has happened, but let's look a bit more closely at *how* it happened.

The followers of Jesus were gathered together, it says, "in one place" (v. 1). In the next verse, when it describes the sound of the Spirit coming, it says that it filled "all the house" where they had been sitting. Cloven tongues like fire came down and rested on each of them (v. 3), and as the Spirit filled them they began to speak in many different languages (v. 4). There were devout men in Jerusalem at that time, as it says, "out of *every nation* under heaven" (v. 5). They were there in

Jerusalem because of the Temple, about which more in a minute. When word of this great miracle got around, a multitude gathered at this *house*, moving away from the Temple, and heard the disciples speaking the wonderful works of God (v. 11) in their own languages.

The Temple complex was huge. Picture a rectangle running north-south, covering about 35 acres. The east side was Solomon's Colonnade (John 10:23; Acts 3:11; 5:12). Part of the retaining wall for the western side still remains today—the famous Wailing Wall. There was a large Pool of Israel outside the north wall, and at the northwest corner was the Antonia Fortress, where 600 soldiers were garrisoned. This was named for Mark Anthony, and Paul gave his impromptu sermon from the stairway up to that fortress from the inside Temple court (Acts 21:40). The south wall was the Royal Stoa, the most ornate part of the complex— where Jesus as a boy had discussed the things of God with the rabbis of Israel (Luke 2:46). The Temple sanctuary and restricted courts butted out from the west wall, and did not quite reach the east wall. Everything inside the walls and outside the central Temple area was the Court of the *Gentiles*.

A sign was posted in the Court of the Gentiles that said, "No foreigner is allowed within the balustrades and embankment about the sanctuary. Whoever is caught will be personally responsible for his ensuing death." The accusation that Paul had violated this law was not a trifling accusation (Acts 21:28). Paul is probably refer-ring to this restricted area when he says that in Christ the wall of partition has been torn down (Eph. 2:14).

As you entered the central Temple area from the east, you went through the Beautiful Gate (Acts 3:2), and came into the Court of the Women. There were also four gates on the north and four on the south side of this court. This is the court where the treasury was (Mark 12:41–44). Proceeding west, you then entered the Court of the Priests. Then came the Holy Place, and after that the Holy of Holies. The internal Temple was plated with gold, and when the sun was shining on it, you could not look directly at it. It was glorious. As they walked through the Temple complex, the dis-ciples of Christ were not rubber-necking for no reason (Matt. 24:1).

So now we come to a strange inversion. If the Shekinah glory were to reappear in Jerusalem, where would you *expect* it to appear? You would expect it to appear the same way it had for Moses at the Tabernacle (Deut. 31:15), or for Solomon at the first Temple (2 Chron. 7:1). But that is not what happened. In order to get to the nondescript, no-name place where it had hap-pened, the multitude had to *leave* the Temple complex.

Not only that, but when the multitude gathered at the new center, the place where the Spirit now was, the new Holy of Holies, what did they hear? They heard the babble of languages from all over tarnation. They heard at the center what they had been hearing only at the periphery before. God had reached down inside Israel, inside the Temple, and pulled everything inside out. The Spirit "got loose" from the Temple, away from His official handlers and representatives. God had now placed Gentile chatter at the new center. Fire rested on each of the disciples, as though each of them were an altar. And the power of the Lord was there.

This was not done arbitrarily or capriciously. The Court of the Gentiles was the place where Jesus had dealt with the moneychangers twice, and where He drove the clean animals (representing Jews) out of the area reserved for the Gentiles (Acts 10:11–17).

What did Jesus say when He did this? He said, "My house shall be called *of all nations* the house of prayer" (Mark 11:15–19). Jesus had visited the House of God officially twice, the same way a priest in the Old Testament was to visit a house with leprosy (Lev. 14:33–48). But if the lesser measures did not suffice, then it was necessary to dismantle the house entirely, which the Romans came and did.

Now when Jesus described the streaks of this particular leprosy, what were the characteristics that He mentioned? There were two: refusal to let the Gentiles approach God in order to pray to Him (for all nations), and grasping avarice and theft (den of thieves). This is why their house was left to them desolate (Matt. 23:38). And what did God accomplish in the new

Temple, assembled out of living stones? How did the
new Temple answer the dual indictment of the old
Temple? The praises of God in every tongue were now
at the center, and the people of God were character-
ized by overflowing generosity (Acts 2:44–45).

Of course the Temple was still in the picture (Acts
2:46), but it was one of the places where believers
would *go* with the Word, and not the anointed place
from which they would *come*.

We, living as we do in the uttermost parts of the
earth (Acts 1:8), might think that the application is
obvious: build churches that are as diverse as a ran-
dom sampling taken from the Court of the Gentiles.
But that is not *quite* it. This is certainly true of the
Church, but all those people were in one place because
of the old system. When the first missionaries got to
Hawaii, they were not welcomed by a committee of
Swedes, Jews, and Eskimos. The message of Pentecost
does not reduce to a spiritual quota system. But at
the same time, we need to recognize that the Holy of
Holies is now everywhere (1 Cor. 3:16). The sanctuary
has not been decentralized, but rather pancentralized.

SUPERSESSIONISM

In the preceding sections, we have seen that the Jews
were chosen by God to model for all the nations what
a covenant relationship with God was like. It is not

that the Gentiles were excluded in the Old Testament, but then, after Jesus came, God suddenly changed His mind. No, the Gentiles had a place in God's redemptive plan from the beginning.

The purpose of this section is to make the case for supersessionism, the idea that the Church is the true Israel now. As Bavinck put it, "The church of Christ is now the true seed of Abraham, the people and the Israel of God."[1]

Before I begin, there is a certain understanding of supersessionism that I don't want to promote. It is not as though God had chosen the Norwegians to be His people, and then one day He changed His mind and selected the Swedes instead. No. There is a real sense in which the faithful Jews of the Old Testament were the bud, and the Christian church is the flower. But there is also a sense in which reversals are taking place. These reversals are experienced by the faithless. For example, Jesus solemnly warned the chief priests and Pharisees that their house, the house they took such pride in, was going to be left to them desolate: "Therefore say I unto you, the kingdom of God shall be taken from you, and given to a nation bringing forth the fruits thereof" (Matt. 21:43).

Whether or not God promised that the Jews would be grafted back in again at the end of history, it is indisputably the case that Gentiles were grafted into

1. Herman Bavinck, *The Wonderful Works of God* (Philadelphia: Westminster Seminary Press, 2020), 500.

the olive tree of the Abrahamic covenant in the first century. "For if thou wert cut out of the olive tree which is wild by nature, and wert graffed contrary to nature into a good olive tree..." (Rom. 11:24a).

This olive tree is a biblical picture of Israel, and this is what Gentiles were grafted into.

> The LORD called thy name, A green olive tree, fair, and of goodly fruit: with the noise of a great tumult he hath kindled fire upon it, and the branches of it are broken. (Jer. 11:16)

> His branches shall spread, And his beauty shall be as the olive tree, And his smell as Lebanon. (Hos. 14:6)

Everyone who has been baptized in the name of the Father, Son, and Holy Spirit has been thereby grafted into Christ. And one of the consequences of belonging to Christ is that by virtue of that baptism you become part of the seed of Abraham. Again, this is explicitly stated: "There is neither Jew nor Greek, there is neither bond nor free, there is neither male nor female: for ye are all one in Christ Jesus. And if ye be Christ's, then are ye Abraham's seed, and heirs according to the promise" (Gal. 3:28–29).

In order to be a true Jew, you need to have a circumcised heart. If you do not have such a heart, then according to Scripture you are not considered to be a Jew at all. "For he is not a Jew, which is one outwardly; neither is that circumcision, which is outward in the flesh: But he is a Jew, which is one inwardly; and circumcision is that of the heart, in the spirit, and not in the letter; whose praise is not of men, but of God" (Rom. 2:28–29).

Note that Paul says that without such regeneration, a Jew is not a Jew at all. Incidentally, while we are here and arguing by analogy, we must also say that in the same sense unregenerate Christians are not Christians. And if we follow the analogy all the way out, we see Paul using Jew in two senses—ethnic Jews, his kinsmen in the flesh, and genuine spiritual Jews, those who have the faith of Abraham. Thus we might easily be confronted with a Scythian who was a Jew, and another man, of the tribe of Benjamin, circumcised on the eighth day, who claimed to be a Jew, but was actually a member of the synagogue of Satan (Rev. 2:9; 3:9). In the same way today, we can have a baptized infidel who is a Christian in the sense that he is not a Buddhist, but who would fall under the same kind of condemnation that Paul offers here at the end of Romans 2. "He is not a Christian who is one outwardly; neither is that baptism which is outward and applied to the body. But he is a Christian who is one inwardly, and baptism is of the heart, in the spirit."

This idea that the church is Israel now is not some esoteric doctrine, tucked away in an obscure corner of the Scriptures somewhere. It is everywhere assumed in all the basic Christian doctrines. The name of our holy book is the New Testament. That New Testament is defined in terms of the previous testament, the Old Testament, which was the possession of Israel.

Jesus instituted the Last Supper, and referred to the cup that He raised as the cup of "the new covenant in my blood." This new covenant in His blood is the covenant that was promised by the great Jeremiah. And that covenant was made with whom? "Behold, the days come, saith the LORD, that I will make a new covenant with the *house of Israel*, and with the *house of Judah*" (Jer. 31:31).

This means that every Christian who partakes of the Lord's Supper, regardless of how many Norwegians were unearthed by his AncestryDNA tests, is claiming to be a part of the true Israel of God. The new covenant is with Israel and with Judah. Unless we Gentiles have been incorporated into that Israel, we have no part in it.

Not only can God bring Gentiles into Israel generally, He can even bring them into particular tribes, thus qualifying them for ministry. "I will gather all nations and tongues; And they shall come, and see my glory... And they shall declare my glory among the Gentiles... And I will also take of them for priests and for Levites, saith the LORD" (Isa. 66:18–21).

In the Old Testament, the Jews were told that Jerusalem was the place where God placed His name. "So king Rehoboam strengthened himself in Jerusalem, and reigned: for Rehoboam was one and forty years old when he began to reign, and he reigned seventeen years *in Jerusalem, the city which the* LORD *had chosen out of all the tribes of Israel, to put his name there*" (2 Chron. 12:13).

Christians are citizens of a new Jerusalem, and a new Jerusalem means a new Israel. "But Jerusalem which is above is free, which is the mother of us all" (Gal. 4:26).

As Christians gather on the Lord's Day for worship, where do we assemble? "But ye are come unto mount Sion, and unto the city of the living God, the heavenly Jerusalem, and to an innumerable company of angels" (Heb. 12:22).

All of this sounds pretty Jewish to me.

There are many other ways to make this point, but to avoid becoming tedious, I will settle for just one more. Israel was entrusted with the vineyard of God— in a very real sense, they *were* the vineyard of God. But according to God's evaluation, they greatly abused the stewardship that was entrusted to them.

> Now will I sing to my wellbeloved a song of my
> beloved touching his vineyard. My wellbeloved
> hath a vineyard in a very fruitful hill: And he

fenced it, and gathered out the stones thereof, and planted it with the choicest vine, and built a tower in the midst of it, and also made a wine-press therein: and he looked that it should bring forth grapes, and it brought forth wild grapes. And now, O inhabitants of Jerusalem, and men of Judah, judge, I pray you, betwixt me and my vineyard. What could have been done more to my vineyard, that I have not done in it? wherefore, when I looked that it should bring forth grapes, brought it forth wild grapes? And now go to; I will tell you what I will do to my vineyard: I will take away the hedge thereof, and it shall be eaten up; and break down the wall thereof, and it shall be trodden down: And I will lay it waste: it shall not be pruned, nor digged; but there shall come up briers and thorns: I will also command the clouds that they rain no rain upon it. For the vineyard of the LORD of hosts is the house of Israel, and the men of Judah his pleasant plant: and he looked for judgment, but behold oppression; for righteousness, but behold a cry. (Isa. 5:1–7)

With this as the backdrop, we can better understand what was happening when the Lord Jesus told the parable of the rebellious vintners, the ones who mistreated their master's messengers, even killing some, and then finally killing the master's son so that the "inheritance may be ours" (Luke 20:14). The chief priests and scribes plotted against Jesus as a consequence because "they perceived that he had spoken this parable against them" (Luke 20:19).

And what was the judgment going to be? "He shall come and destroy these husbandmen, *and shall give the vineyard to others.* And when they heard it, they said, God forbid" (Luke 20:16).

Christianity is not a faith that was developed from scratch. Christians have always rested their New Testament on the foundation of the Old Testament. This means that we have always considered ourselves to be in some sense the true heirs of the promises God made to His people. And this means that consistent Christians must always be supersessionists of some stripe.

CHAPTER 8
Children of Hagar

·AS DEFINED EARLIER, THE SUPER-
sessionist position is that "the church is Israel now." All
the promises of the Old Testament have come to fruition in Jesus Christ (2 Cor. 1:20), and hence, all who
are in Christ have been brought into the true Israel of
God. Unbelieving Jews have been cut out of that true
Israel, and believing Gentiles have been brought into
it. "That at that time ye were without Christ, being
aliens from the commonwealth of Israel, and strangers
from the covenants of promise, having no hope, and
without God in the world" (Eph. 2:12).

In other words, we Gentiles used to be outside Israel and were aliens, but through the blood of Christ we have been brought near.

But there is a difference between what might be called the hard supersessionist position and the soft supersessionist position. The hard supersessionist holds that when the Jews were excluded from their previous position of privilege as Israel, then that was *it* for them. According to this thinking, they no longer have any special status in the redemptive plan of God at all. They are on the same footing as any other unbelieving tribe or group. When they are converted, it will usher in no golden age. It is the key to nothing. It will be a glad event, of course, but it has nothing to do with God's prophetic timetable. The future history of the world is not connected to the future history of the Jews.

In contrast, the soft supersessionist agrees that the church is Israel now, and that ethnic Israel is currently not a part of the true Israel. And when it comes to the salvation of individual Jews currently, we also agree that an unbelieving Jew is in the same position as an unbelieving Irishman, or Chinese, or Navajo. But the soft supersessionist holds that the Jews as a people are still part of God's purpose and plan for the world. The gifts and calling of God are irrevocable. When the Jews are converted en masse, this will usher in the latter day glory, and the resurrection of the dead. In short, the status of the Jews with regard to faith and unbelief is relevant for the rest of the world. As some have probably guessed, the arguments presented in this book are coming from a soft supersessionist position.

Now one of the questions that will naturally be asked is what covenantal category these severed Jewish branches could possibly have in the meantime. The Gentiles who were grafted in are described as "wild" olive branches, distinct from cultivated olive branches. But the excised Jews are simply cut out—and they are not specifically described as being grafted into a wild olive tree. If they are just a tangled pile of debris next to the field where the olive tree is located, then how could they remain alive? More than that, how could they remain alive (thus providing graftable branches) for two millennia or more?

We don't ever want analogies to take us captive, even if they are biblical analogies. We don't want to press them too far, in other words. But I do think we are given a clue as to the covenantal status of unbelieving Jews, a clue given to us in Galatians.

> For it is written, that Abraham had two sons, the one by a bondmaid, the other by a freewoman. But he who was of the bondwoman was born after the flesh; but he of the freewoman was by promise. Which things are an allegory: for these are the two covenants; the one from the mount Sinai, which gendereth to bondage, which is

Agar. For this Agar is mount Sinai in Arabia, and answereth to Jerusalem which now is, and is in bondage with her children. But Jerusalem which is above is free, which is the mother of us all. For it is written, Rejoice, thou barren that bearest not; break forth and cry, thou that travailest not: for the desolate hath many more children than she which hath an husband. (Gal. 4:22-27)

Although the ethnic Jews are descended from Abraham *physically*, covenantally speaking, they are Ishmaelites. Summed up, they are in a covenant of bondage. However disciplined and hardworking they are, they do not know the taste of grace. They are driven, but not liberated. They are not children of the free woman, but rather through unbelief they have made themselves children of the slave concubine.

And if you read to the end of Galatians 4, you can see that Paul argues forcefully that the Jews are therefore to be put out of Abraham's household. They do not belong there—because the indicator of Abrahamic blood is faith, and faith alone. "Nevertheless what saith the scripture? Cast out the bondwoman and her son: for the son of the bondwoman shall not be heir with the son of the freewoman. So then, brethren, we are not children of the bondwoman, but of the free" (Gal. 4:30-31).

Realizing that while we are not mixing metaphors, we are in fact *juggling* metaphors. We have the

illustration from Abraham's family, with the unbelieving Jews as children of the slave concubine. We also
have a horticultural illustration, with the unbelieving
Jews as pruned branches.

So returning to the image of the olive tree, we may
take the liberty of expanding the illustration slightly. Paul
assumes that the Gentile nations were wild olive trees—
but at least they were alive and growing someplace. This
would lead me to think that when the unbelieving Jews
were cut out of the olive tree, they were not thrown onto a
gigantic burn pile. Rather I envision them as being a tree
of Ishmael, planted in the clearing in between the wild
olive trees on the hillside, and the cultivated Abrahamic
tree in the middle of the garden of the Master.

If the Jews, after the destruction of Jerusalem, had
simply disappeared from the face of the earth, as many
other people groups have done, we wouldn't be faced
with this problem. Nobody thinks much today about
what to do with the Sumerians or Hittites. But the fact
that the Jews are still here means that we must incor-
porate them into Paul's illustration somehow.

They are not in the same position as the Greeks for
the same reason that a woman you divorced is not in
the same category as a woman you never married. At
the same time, she is no longer a wife. It can even be
said that she is no longer even a concubine.

But this is not the end of the story. If as John the
Baptist taught, God can make children of Abraham out

of rocks and stones (Matt. 3:9), then He most certainly can make children of Abraham out of people who used to be children of Abraham. In fact, in various places, He promises to do so. "Yet the number of the children of Israel shall be as the sand of the sea, which cannot be measured nor numbered; and it shall come to pass, that in the place where it was said unto them, Ye are not my people, there it shall be said unto them, Ye are the sons of the living God" (Hos. 1:10).

IRREVOCABLE GIFTS

What I would like to do next is address an intramural debate among postmillennialists regarding the future conversion of the Jews. In Romans 11, the apostle Paul makes a prediction concerning the future of Israel "according to the flesh." Postmillennialists are divided about what constitutes the fulfillment of that prophecy.

One group of postmillennialists sides with the majority opinion of Reformed theology, which holds that this prophecy of Israel's conversion to Christ has not yet been fulfilled, and so (regarding this prophecy), they are futurists. A more recent view, held by men like James Jordan and Peter Leithart (and a handful of old-timers, like Cotton Mather), holds that this prediction was indeed fulfilled after Paul made it, but it was fulfilled a long time in *our* past—shortly before the destruction of the Temple in AD 70. This is the preterist view of this particular prediction.

Now it should be obvious that this has great relevance for how we think of the Jews today. For the preterists, the Jews of today have no unique place in God's economy of redemption at all. They will eventually come to Christ (this is a debate among postmillennialists, after all), but when they come to Christ they will be in exactly the same position as any other tribe or nation. As Jordan has put it, "What is the purpose for there to be a continuing people of Israel distinct from the rest of the Kingdom? And the answer is that there is no purpose at all. Post-biblical Jews are simply one people group among all the rest."[1]

But for the futurists, while they hold that Jews today are lost without Christ, they believe the Jews still have a key role to play in the history of redemption. On the basis of Paul's prediction in Romans 11, futurists hold that a future conversion of the Jews will unlock a massive blessing for the entire world. Paul's argument is that if their rejection of Christ was such a great blessing for the Gentiles, what will their repentance be but life from the dead? The overarching idea is that the gospel will spread inexorably to all the nations of men, which will all be gradually converted. Finally Israel, one of

1. James Jordan, response to "Judah's Life from the Dead" by Tim Gallant, in *The Glory of Kings*, eds. Peter J. Leithart and John Barach (Eugene, OR: Pickwick Publications, 2011), 53.

the last holdouts, will repent and come to Christ, and this will be "life from the dead." The rejection of Israel leads to the fulness of the Gentiles, which in turn leads to the fulness of Israel, which ushers in the latter-day glory, when the lion will eat straw like an ox.

This is why the "conversion of the Jews" has played such a key role in historic Reformed thought, and has made its way into the common phrases of everyday life. It even shows up in Andrew Marvell's poem "To His Coy Mistress":

> I would
> Love you ten years before the flood,
> And you should, if you please, refuse
> Till the conversion of the Jews.

In the Westminster Larger Catechism, Question 191 asks what we pray for when we pray for the kingdom to come. Among other things, we pray for "the gospel [to be] propagated throughout the world, the Jews called, [and] the fulness of the Gentiles brought in." Again, this has been the generally received understanding of Romans 11 in the Reformed world.[2]

But another received understanding of the Reformed world is that synods and councils can screw things up. As the Westminster Confession puts it, "All

2. See Appendix 2.

synods or councils, since the Apostles' times, whether general or particular, may err; and many have erred" (WCF 31.4).

When confronted with a broad and agreed-upon consensus, we should *still* be able to say "to the law and to the testimony." So let's look at what the Scriptures teach about this.

My first argument against the preterist view of Romans 11 is that it is necessarily pretty bleak. The words of the promise are glorious, and fill us with hope. "Life from the dead." "Fullness of the Gentiles." "All Israel shall be saved." "God will turn away ungodliness from Jacob." To be told that this has already been fulfilled in history, and in such a way that nobody noticed it, or remarked on it, or wrote it down, and that it made no kind of a dent at all, is kind of a small beer fulfillment. It really is thin soup. It is profoundly anticlimactic. It is as though a preacher read out this glorious text from Isaiah—"And in this mountain shall the LORD of hosts make unto all people a feast of fat things, a feast of wines on the lees, of fat things full of marrow, of wines on the lees well refined" (Isa. 25:6)—in order to present his argument that this was to be fulfilled at the first introduction of the chocolate fountain for the Sunday brunch at the Golden Corral. It makes me think of that old Gahan Wilson cartoon, with a group of men standing around in nondescript robes, with halos stuck on the backs of their heads, a whiskey bottle on the ground, plaster falling off the wall, the E of HEAVEN over the gate fallen over—and the caption was, "Somehow I thought the whole thing would be a lot classier."

Hymenaeus and Philetus taught that the resurrection was past already (2 Tim. 2:18), and this means that any people who believed them would need to ratchet their expectations downwards somewhat. I mean, to look at the suffering of the present world and to tell yourself that we have already achieved the apex of human happiness . . . well, that would be a hard sell. Picture Hymenaeus struggling to get through the Q & A at the end of his talk, because a homeless guy in the back won't sit down and keeps saying, "You mean this is *it*?"

It is the same kind of thing here. When we go through the book of Romans carefully, we see that Paul has promised us the sun, moon, and stars. Abraham was promised that he would be heir of the world (Rom. 4:13), and that it wouldn't be through the law, but rather through the righteousness of faith. We need to believe *up* to the promises rather than lowering the promises *down* to our levels of quasi-unbelief.

And when Paul gets to the promises of Romans 11, he doesn't let up any. Verse 15 echoes Ezekiel 37:9 in the Septuagint, where the prophet is used to bring about a *monumental* transformation: "So I prophesied as he commanded me, and the breath came into them, and they lived, and stood up upon their feet, *an exceeding great army*" (Ezek. 37:10).

Paul teaches us that eye has not seen and ear has not heard. What? What has not ever entered into the heart of man? The answer is, "the things which God hath prepared for them that love him" (1 Cor. 2:9). In the face of this kind of statement, do we really want to represent the Scriptures as overpromising and underdelivering?

My second argument is this. Whenever the removal of the Jews' hard rejection of Christ happens, it needs to happen *after* the fulness of the Gentiles has come in. The order of events is plain: "For I would not, brethren, that ye should be ignorant of this mystery, lest ye should be wise in your own conceits; that blindness in part is happened to Israel, until the fulness of the Gentiles be come in" (Rom. 11:25).

If the blindness of the Jews had been removed by AD 70, the fullness of the Gentiles must have happened *before* that. But in the first century, although Christ had been preached in many places throughout the Roman Empire (Col. 1:6, 23), the church was by no means established everywhere. It seems to me extraordinarily difficult for a *postmillennialist* to argue that the conditions at the end of the first century were anything close to the fullness of the Gentiles having come in.

According to Rodney Stark's most reasonable calculations, there were about 7,500 Christians by the end of the first century. That is 0.0126 percent of an estimated 60 million people in the Roman world.[3] Is *that* what we are talking about when we refer to the fullness of the Gentiles, along with all the Jews who presumably came into the church at that time? That's it? This puts me in mind of the Golden Corral again.

Even if we think that Stark's number is low (based on the numbers at the beginning of the book of Acts), it still doesn't touch the argument. Multiply his number by ten, and we are still talking about a minuscule fraction of the Roman world. How could that be the fullness of the Gentiles? And given that this debate is happening between postmillennialists, all of whom believe that the earth is one day going to be as full of the knowledge of the Lord as the waters cover the sea, why on earth would we look back at a time when it was nothing of the kind, and say *that* was the fullness of the Gentiles?

Finally, this promise is one of the necessary preconditions that Scripture assigns for the Final Coming of Christ. According to the divine clock, when Israel turns in repentance to the Lord, fully and completely, then the end will come.

Let's look at this in several passages outside Romans 11 that make the same point.

3. Rodney Stark, *The Rise of Christianity* (Princeton: Princeton University Press, 1996), 7.

> Behold, your house is left unto you desolate. For
> I say unto you, Ye shall not see me henceforth,
> till ye shall say, Blessed is he that cometh in the
> name of the Lord. (Matt. 23:38–39)

Jesus has just finished His lament over Jerusalem, and this is right before His long description of the terrible judgments that were going to come down upon that hapless nation. In short, the Jews—whose house is currently being left desolate—will not see the Lord until they bless His name. And when they bless His name, then He will appear.

After Peter healed the lame man at the Beautiful Gate, he found an opportunity to address the "men of *Israel*" (Acts 3:12). What does he say?

> Repent ye therefore, and be converted, that
> your sins may be blotted out, when the times
> of refreshing shall come from the presence of
> the Lord; And he shall send Jesus Christ, which
> before was preached unto you: Whom the
> heaven must receive until the times of restitu-
> tion of all things, which God hath spoken by the
> mouth of all his holy prophets since the world
> began. (Acts 3:19–21)

Peter calls on the men of Israel to repent and be converted so that three things might then happen: the blotting out of their sins, the times of refreshing coming from the presence of the Lord, and last, that the Lord might send Jesus Christ back again (Acts 1:11). To repeat, he says that the men of Israel should repent so that Christ might return. The repentance of Israel is the final trigger that will inaugurate the end of all things.

And this is precisely why the hardened unbelief of Israel was such a mercy for the Gentiles. If the whole nation of Israel had repented after Pentecost, that would have ushered in the End, and that would have been *it*. This is why Romans 11 says *four times* that the unbelief of Israel was the basis for the Gentiles' salvation.

> Through their fall salvation is come unto the Gentiles. (11:11)
>
> The fall of them be the riches of the world, and the diminishing of them the riches of the Gentiles. (11:12)
>
> The casting away of them [is] the reconciling of the world. (11:15)
>
> [The Gentiles] have now obtained mercy through their unbelief. (11:30)

We may sum all this up by saying that the Gentiles received salvation and mercy *because* the Jews had rejected it. I agree with the assessment of Tim Gallant that this is difficult to make sense of unless Scripture teaches that the belief of Israel would trigger the last stage of human history.[4] In other words, the Jews' hardness of heart carved out a temporal space in which it became possible for the Gentiles to be saved.

BOAST NOT AGAINST THE BRANCHES

One of the reasons why the monarchical episcopacy developed in the church by the second century is because (on a worldly level) some churches are more important than others. If you are the pastor of a small community church out in the sticks, and your congregation consists of six farmers, their wives, and the owner of the feed store, then you are not going to get the same recognition as a man who pastors a church in the D.C. area, where senators frequently attend, and the president sometimes. Now we should all be biblically aware enough to know that what is honorable in the sight of man is not necessarily the same in the eyes of God (Luke 16:15). We all realize that there are obscure pastors who are great in the kingdom, and famous pastors who are not.

Nevertheless, the churches in important cities need to take care that they guard themselves against

4. Tim Gallant, "Salvation of Gentile and Jew: The Eschatological Significance of Israel's Future Restoration," https://timgallant.com/essays /SalvationGentileAndJew.pdf.

a worldly flattery, and the church at Rome was located in the most important city in the world. Paul had seen the first stirrings of a conceit there that was going to cause a lot of trouble down the road, and he was at distinct pains to warn them about it.

In the Reformation, we recovered the truth of election, which assured the saints that no one can lay a charge against God's elect—it is God who justifies (Rom. 8:33). But the Roman Catholic Church taught that no one's salvation was secure until they were dead and in Heaven. Ten minutes before the heart attack, if a cardinal or a pope committed a mortal sin, then he was consigned to the flames. But the Catholic dogma was also that the Church at Rome itself could not fall away—*its* position was eternally secure. This was the reverse of what the Protestants taught. According to the Protestants, any lampstand could be removed from any church (Rev. 2:5), but the elect individual was untouchable. For the Roman church, there was no such thing as eternal security for any individual in this life, but the church would always remain the church.

Now the apostle Paul contradicts this Roman dogma, and he does so, quite strikingly, in his letter *to the Church at Rome*. He saw this error coming, in other words. It was already taking shape in his day.

With regard to the elect individual, his words are stirring: "Who shall lay any thing to the charge of God's elect? It is God that justifieth" (Rom. 8:33). And with regard to the status of the church generally, his warning is quite sobering. "Boast not against the branches. But if thou boast, thou bearest not the root, but the root thee. Well; because of unbelief they were broken off, and thou standest by faith. Be not highminded, but fear: For if God spared not the natural branches, take heed lest he also spare not thee" (Rom. 11:20–21).

The Jews had stumbled because of a covenantal and ethnic presumption, and Paul cautions the Gentile Romans against committing the very same sin. What happened to the Sanhedrin at Jerusalem could certainly happen to the See of Rome. And why? Rome did not support the root, but rather the root Rome, and faith alone kept the sap flowing.

And this explains what Romans 9–11 is doing in the book of Romans in the first place. At the end of chapter 8, Paul had flown up to majestic heights. If you are the elect of God, absolutely *nothing* can separate you from the love of God which is in Christ Jesus (Rom. 8:38–39).

So how do you explain the Jews then? They were the elect nation (Isa. 45:4), and they were expending more than a little energy trying to kill the apostle Paul, as they had in fact killed the Elect One of God (Isa. 42:1), their own Messiah. It sure seems like something had separated *them* from the love of God.

This section of Romans is Paul explaining the place of the Jews in God's economy of salvation. Elect individual saints are predestined to be conformed to the final image of Christ. The olive tree, spanning centuries, and including Old and New Covenants both, is also eternally secure. But branches can be both cut out and grafted in.

The Roman Gentiles had just been grafted in, and they were looking with some disdain at the pile of unbelieving Jewish branches that had been cut out, apparently to make room for them. And this is where Paul says "boast not against the branches." This is the word that antisemites everywhere need to take to heart—and many of them need to be pierced to the heart first. Boast not against the Jews. Boast not against the unbelieving Jews. Boast not against the Jews who were plotting against Paul. And why? Because they still have a role to play. There is a *reason* why Paul says the gifts and calling of God are irrevocable (Rom. 11:29).

The promises given to Israel in the Old Testament were ironclad.

> Thus saith the LORD, which giveth the sun for a
> light by day, and the ordinances of the moon and
> of the stars for a light by night, which divideth
> the sea when the waves thereof roar; The LORD
> of hosts is his name: If those ordinances depart
> from before me, saith the LORD, then the seed of
> Israel also shall cease from being a nation before

> me for ever. Thus saith the LORD; If heaven
> above can be measured, and the foundations of
> the earth searched out beneath, I will also cast off
> all the seed of Israel for all that they have done,
> saith the LORD. (Jer. 31:35–37)

God kept those promises by keeping the tree secure, grafting in new branches, and promising the native and natural branches a place in the tree again—which is going to come, through faith in Christ.

This is how Paul can make such dramatic statements about the future blessedness that awaits Israel. Earlier in his argument, he had shown us that Israel according to the promises must receive the blessings (by definition), but here he is saying that Israel according to the flesh will be included in them as well. How so? How is this possible?

> And they also, if they abide not still in unbelief,
> shall be graffed in: for God is able to graff them
> in again. For if thou wert cut out of the olive tree
> which is wild by nature, and wert graffed contrary
> to nature into a good olive tree: how much more
> shall these, which be the natural branches, be
> graffed into their own olive tree?
>
> For I would not, brethren, that ye should be
> ignorant of this mystery, lest ye should be wise
> in your own conceits; that blindness in part

is happened to Israel, until the fulness of the
Gentiles be come in. And so all Israel shall be
saved: as it is written, There shall come out of
Sion the Deliverer, and shall turn away ungodliness from Jacob: For this is my covenant unto
them, when I shall take away their sins. As concerning the gospel, they are enemies for your
sakes: but as touching the election, they are
beloved for the father's sakes. For the gifts and
calling of God are without repentance. For as ye
in times past have not believed God, yet have
now obtained mercy through their unbelief:
Even so have these also now not believed, that
through your mercy they also may obtain mercy.
For God hath concluded them all in unbelief, that he might have mercy upon all. (Rom.
11:23–32)

Paul begins with a conditional statement, on the
human level. If Israel repents of its unbelief, then God
is certainly able to graft them in again (v. 23). Just
consider the nature of the case. If wild olive branches
could be grafted in, then how much more could severed natural branches be grafted in (v. 24)? Makes
sense, right?

But Paul then moves from the logical possibilities
to the prophetic necessities. He does not want the
Romans to be ignorant of this mystery (Paul's common

word for something prophesied in the Old Testament and made manifest in the New). The partial blindness of Israel (excluding the remnant) was predicted until the fullness of the Gentiles had been reached (v. 25). And knowing this would keep the Gentiles from getting conceited about Israel's ongoing exclusion (v. 25). Notice that Paul's whole reason for going into this is to prevent an antisemitic sentiment from growing up among them. So then Paul cites one of the places that tells us about all of this (v. 26)—which was from Isaiah 59:20–21 and Isaiah 27:9.

As we consider Romans 11:24–26, it is crucial to note that the referent of the word *Israel* does not change. Let me quote those verses, and then render an amplified form of them, drawing on Isaiah 59 and 27, and the larger context found in Isaiah.

For if thou wert cut out of the olive tree which is wild by nature, and wert graffed contrary to nature into a good olive tree: how much more shall these, which be the natural branches, be graffed into their own olive tree? For I would not, brethren, that ye should be ignorant of this mystery, lest ye should be wise in your own conceits; that blindness in part is happened to Israel, until the fulness of the Gentiles be come in. And so all Israel shall be saved: as it is written, There shall come out of Sion the Deliverer, and shall turn away ungodliness from Jacob. (Rom. 11:24–26)

Here is my amplified (and paraphrased) version:

> For if you Gentiles were cut out of your natu-
> rally wild olive tree, and were grafted contrary
> to nature into a good olive tree, how much more
> shall these Israelites, who are natural branches,
> be grafted back into the stock of their own olive
> tree? Brothers, I do not wish you to be ignorant
> of this mystery, lest you become wise in your own
> conceits—a partial blindness has happened to
> Israel until the fulness of the Gentiles is gathered
> in. And so all Israel shall be saved, as it is written,
> "A Deliverer shall arise in Zion, and Gentiles shall
> come to that light, and kings to that brightness,
> and shall turn away ungodliness from Jacob.
> Jacob will be cleansed, Israel will blossom and
> bud, and fill the face of the world with fruit—
> Egypt will come, and Assyria, and will worship
> the Lord." (Rom. 11:24-26)

After the Deliverer arises in Zion (Isa. 59:20), the
Gentiles come to the light (Isa. 60:3). *After* the guilt of
Jacob is removed (Isa. 27:9), Egypt and Assyria come
to worship the Lord on the mountain of the Lord. The
New Testament frequently maintains the distinctions
of various Old Testament texts, bringing them over.
It is true that Gentiles are brought into the commonwealth of Israel (Eph. 2:12), but not in a way that
forgets where the branches came from. Some were
cultivated and some were wild.

We see an example of this kind of distinction between Jew and Gentile in Genesis 12. Abraham is promised that he will become the father of a "great nation." The primary referent of that would be Israel. But he is also promised that a blessing is going to come to all the other families of the earth, *distinct* from Israel. Now we are taught in the New Testament that the way these families of the earth will receive that promised blessing is through incorporation into the great olive tree of faith.

God has made one new man out of the two (Eph. 2:15), but they were two when the promises were first made concerning them. "And I will make of thee a great nation, and I will bless thee, and make thy name great; and thou shalt be a blessing: And I will bless them that bless thee, and curse him that curseth thee: and in thee shall all families of the earth be blessed" (Gen. 12:2–3).

It is granted that eventually (after centuries) the wild ones will be indistinguishable from the cultivated olive branches, which is why Paul was at such pains to explain to them this mystery. Why did Paul go into such detail with the *Roman* church?

Remember they were the church in the capital of a great and powerful empire. There had been a large number of unbelieving branches with an ancient pedigree that had been removed in order to "make room" for these Roman branches. He even puts that argument into their mouths (v. 19). Paul says that he brought this whole thing up—and his expression is quite striking—"lest ye be wise in your own conceits" (v. 25).

He did all of this because he was heading off a primitive seed form of antisemitism—believing Gentiles vaunting themselves over against unbelieving Jews. But his command is explicit: "Boast not against the branches" (v. 18). "Be not high-minded but fear" (v. 20).

Antisemitism is therefore nothing less than disobedience to an express apostolic command.

God's covenant with Israel was that He would take away their sins (v. 27). So, *only for the time being*, the Jews are enemies of the Gentile Christians, because of the gospel. But as concerns election, they are still beloved for their fathers' sake (v. 28). How long will this last? There is a promise that makes their status irrevocable—which is why the Jews will in fact return to Christ (v. 29). The Gentiles used to be mired in unbelief, but were brought out of it by the unbelief of the Jews (v. 30). And then, in a reverse twist, God is going to bring the Jews out of their unbelief through the mercy that was shown to the Gentiles (v. 31). Put this all together, and we see that concluding the Jews in unbelief (for now) was the first move in His plan to bring mercy to the whole world—Jews included (v. 32).

The unbelief of Israel brought the Gentiles in, and the belief of the Gentiles is going to bring the Jews back in.

Now Paul says that all of this is a prophetic mystery, now revealed, and revealed *in order that Gentiles would not become conceited*. Salvation is from the Jews (Jn 4:22), and always will be.

Let's look at how it works. The prophet Isaiah laments the condition of man. Our iniquities have separated us from God (Isa. 59:2). This detestable condition is applied by the apostle Paul to all men, to Gentiles and Jews alike (Rom. 3:15-17; Isa. 59:7-8). Everything falters; everything fails. There is no soundness anywhere. All men are in need of a Savior. When God saw this, when He saw that there was no man, He sent a man—He sent a Deliverer (Isa. 59:16). This great warrior will put on His panoply—the armor of Jesus (Isa. 59:17). Remind you of anything?

Of course—this is the whole armor of God (Eph. 6:11). Put on the whole armor of God therefore (Eph. 6:13-17), which is another way of saying that we are to put on the Lord Jesus Christ. But what does Jesus do in this armor, back in Isaiah?

First, He judges the wicked (Isa. 59:18). As a result, the Gentiles stream to Him. They shall "fear the name of the Lord from the west, and his glory from the rising of the sun" (Isa. 59:19). The world will gather to Him, and He will save them. And then the Redeemer shall come to Zion—and this is the place Paul quotes with reference to his brethren in the flesh, collating it with Isaiah 27:9. The covenant is that Israel's sins will

144   AMERICAN MILK AND HONEY

be forgiven, and this is equated with the Spirit never departing from the mouths of all their descendants (Isa. 59:21). And this brings Isaiah 27 into the mix as well. "Jacob shall take root" and "Israel shall blossom and bud, and fill the face of the world with fruit" (Isa. 27:6). And when the Jews return to Christ, this event will be just as public and as visible as their rejection of Him was. Glory to God, and may He hasten that day.

With regard to the role they have to play in all of this, the gifts and calling for Israel really are irrevocable. God has, in His wisdom and providence, tied the fortunes of the world to the fortunes of the Jews. The apostasy of the Jews opened wide the door of salvation for the Gentiles, and their eventual conversion will be a blessing for them (of course), along with the remainder of the Gentiles. This is a decision that God will never repent of—this is the mystery that He has revealed, and which we are called to live out.

Now this means that it is not possible to be in sync with the purposes of God in this world without loving the Jewish people. Christians who fall prey to antisemitism are trying to disrupt the grace of God for the whole world. It is counterproductive; it is anti-gospel. Gentiles who start boasting over against Jews are ignoring the plain warnings that Paul left for us. Boast not against the branches.

At the same time, as other portions of this book make plain, loving the Jews as God does, for the sake of their fathers, is not the same thing as approving of whatever the Jews might do, or agreeing with Zionism, or agreeing with the present position of the current administration of the Israeli government, whatever it might happen to be. That is not the point. The point is that a peculiar animus against the Jews is out, and to give way to it is to rebel against God's gospel strategy.

One might say "what about the Palestinian Christians that Israel has killed?" Look, this teaching comes from Paul, who was willing to be damned for the sake of the Jews (Rom. 9:3). And he maintained this attitude while outlining their various hypocrisies throughout the book of Romans, and while in full knowledge of the fact that they were trying to kill him.

Mercy to the Gentiles has been God's game plan for bringing mercy to the Jews, and mercy to the Jews is what He is going to use to bring about "life from the dead" for everyone (Rom. 11:15). And so what we are called to do is preach God's mercy in Christ to all the nations with a view toward cultural transformation, and to live it out in such a way that the Jews want to get themselves some of that. Personal conversion, certainly, planting of churches, even more. We need to be rebuilding Christendom, and doing so in a way that leaves the doors wide open for the Jews.

One of the great failures of the first Christendom was at just this point, and it is something we have to address. We are called to provoke emulation (11:14); we are not called to *be* envious.

Just as the Jews leave an empty chair for Elijah at their Passover celebrations, so we need to leave a chair empty for them.

CHAPTER 9

Deuteronomic Blessings

ONE OF THE REASONS THAT CHRISTIANS get into a muddle about how their sanctification should look is that they don't know how to fit the blessings of the material world into it. Not only does the resultant confusion cause consternation regarding individual choices about life, it also interferes with our understanding of God's appointed plans for evangelizing the world. Instead of seeking to be grateful to God for His manifest blessings, we have adopted a quasi-pagan view of spirit and matter, relegating God's blessing to an upper-story spiritual realm somewhere. In doing this, we have forgotten how God has determined to guide, discipline, and instruct the world.

But just because we have left material blessings out of our thinking, they do not therefore disappear from the world. Somebody is always going to be better off. And when that happens, our evaluation of it will either be governed by the laws of gratitude, which are biblical, or by the laws of envy, which are demonic. Because Christians have not studied how covenant prosperity works, they have opened the door to all manner of biting, striving, scratching, and carping, and have thus unwittingly created an opportunity for antisemitism to arise. That connection might startle at first, and seem like a leap, but it should become clearer shortly.

BUT AREN'T MATERIAL BLESSINGS AN OLD TESTAMENT THING?

When Christians opt for a dualistic framework, separating the spiritual from the material, they often do this in the name of an Old and New Testament dichotomy. According to this thinking, God promised His people, the Jews, material blessings in the Old Testament as a sort of audiovisual aid for Christians to use in later centuries. And He promises His people now, the Christians, spiritual blessings in the New. Thus, the Jews got Canaan and we get Heaven. The Jews got gold and silver and we get spiritual gold and silver. The Jews got rain for their crops, and we get the latter rain in our souls.

But the reality is a bit more complicated than that. Let's illustrate this with one of the foundational Deuteronomic blessings. "Honour thy father and thy mother, as the LORD thy God hath commanded thee; that thy days may be prolonged, and that it may go well with thee, in the land which the LORD thy God giveth thee" (Deut. 5:16).

This is a command with a promise, and the command was delivered to the children of Israel, gathered around the base of Sinai. The commandment had a promise attached to it, and the promise referred to things "going well" for them in the land of Canaan, which lay before them, awaiting their conquest. God was telling the Jews that if they kept this commandment by honoring father and mother in Canaan, then their lives would be prosperous in the land (of Canaan) which God was giving to them. Pretty straightforward so far.

Paul pointed out that this commandment is the first one that has a promise annexed to it. But he delivered this point, not to Jews, but to a bunch of Gentile kids in Ephesus. And the inheritance they were promised was much greater than the land of Canaan. "Children, obey your parents in the Lord: for this is right. Honour thy father and mother; (which is the first commandment with promise;) That it may be well with thee, and thou mayest live long on the earth" (Eph. 6:1–3).

In short, God's method for promising a blessing in this world to Gentile kids was by means of the promise He made of a blessing in Canaan to Jewish kids.

Notice that God is not promising the Ephesian kids a prospect in Heaven when they die. He is telling them that their life will be long on the *earth*, in *this world*. I mean, at the very least, the promise had to be expanded to Asia Minor, where Ephesus was. And who would dare to say that the promise is somehow annulled for Christian children in Australia, or Japan, or the UK, or America? Who would dare to say that God's offer of this kindness has expired?

But this is momentous. It means that Deuteronomic blessings—for this world—are the possession and birthright of the children of Christians, and their children's children. This has ramifications, as we shall see.

Make no mistake. There *is* an upper story. To be absent from the body is to be present with the Lord (2 Cor. 5:8). There is a general resurrection of the dead at the culmination of all human history (Rom. 8:18-19). To live is Christ, to die is gain (Phil. 1:21). To leave true spiritual blessings out of the equation is to place human beings on the level of swine in a sty—with blessings being understood as anything edible that can fit in the mouth, like mash or acorns.

But the gnostic error, the opposite error, is just as filled with unbelief—ungratefully reducing human beings to the level of wraiths, ghosts, and spiritual wisps.

It is not the case that God gave material blessings to the Jews in the Old Testament, while in the New

Covenant, all the blessings have been transported beyond the stars, or somehow vaporized. On this view, God has apparently appointed a team of burly archangels to throw all of our material blessings into a Cosmic Nebulizer, which will turn every last one of them into a very fine spiritual mist, in order to make Heaven idolatry-proof. "And Jesus answered and said, Verily I say unto you, There is no man that hath left house, or brethren, or sisters, or father, or mother, or wife, or children, or lands, for my sake, and the gospel's, but he shall receive an hundredfold now *in this time, houses,* and brethren, and sisters, and mothers, and children, *and lands,* with persecutions; and in the world to come eternal life" (Mark 10:29–30).

Our tendency is to skip straight to the eternal life part. And we should of course hold fast to that. Jesus did promise eternal life. The problem lies in what we skip over. Jesus also promised His dedicated followers that they would receive family, and *houses,* and *lands,* and that they would do so *in this life.*

Now there is a certain kind of compromised Christian for whom the first part of this passage (v. 29) is the "hard saying." The cares of this world and the deceitfulness of riches can and do choke out spiritual interest (Matt. 13:22). Like the rich young ruler, they go away downcast (Luke 18:23). Jesus demands an "all in" sort of discipleship, and a willingness to forsake absolutely *everything* for Him. "So likewise, whosoever he be of you that forsaketh not all that he hath, he cannot be my disciple" (Luke 14:33).

But there is another kind of Christian, a pious, otherworldly kind, for whom the hard saying is actually found in v. 30. It is as hard to give houses and lands to some Christians as it is to take them away from others. Imagine a glorious mansion on one hundred acres on a scenic stretch of the Oregon coast, and then imagine yourself having been assigned the task of giving it to an otherworldly prayer warrior. The Lord wanted him to be in a position to paint some glorious water colors, but only after conducting his prayer walks on the beach. He nevertheless was struggling with the whole concept because the guilt made it difficult to hold the brush.

These different demands are in tension, but it is a tension created by the wayward bent of our hearts. God does give houses and lands to His people, though only to those who, like Job, are willing to hold them before the Lord on an open palm (Job 1:21–22).

BUT THOSE WARNINGS . . .

But didn't Jesus teach us that it is easier for a camel to go through the eye of a needle than for a rich person to make it into the kingdom (Matt. 19:24)? Are not the warnings against the deceitfulness of riches a regular refrain throughout the New Testament? Indeed they are. Our mistake is thinking that there is anything new about this. Such warnings are as much a part of Deuteronomy as are the promises.

> When thou hast eaten and art full, then thou shalt bless the LORD thy God for the good land which he hath given thee. Beware that thou forget not the LORD thy God, in not keeping his commandments, and his judgments, and his statutes, which I command thee this day: Lest when thou hast eaten and art full, and hast built goodly houses, and dwelt therein; And when thy herds and thy flocks multiply, and thy silver and thy gold is multiplied, and all that thou hast is multiplied; Then thine heart be lifted up, and thou forget the LORD thy God, which brought thee forth out of the land of Egypt, from the house of bondage. (Deut. 8:10–14)

The idea that we ought not to give way to the idolatry of covetousness is no New Testament innovation. The problem we are seeking to solve here is at least as old as Abraham's wealth, and almost certainly older.

The challenge is this: how can we hold things in the palm of our hand without those things themselves growing hands that can hold us in a death grip? The Lord promised that we could handle serpents and not be bitten (Mark 16:18), and mammon is certainly one of those serpents.

God *expects* us to get good at handling wealth. Notice the instruction given to Timothy: "Charge them that are rich in this world, that they be not highminded, nor trust in uncertain riches, but in the living God, who giveth us richly all things to enjoy; That they do good, that they be rich in good works, ready to distribute, willing to communicate; Laying up in store for themselves a good foundation against the time to come, that they may lay hold on eternal life" (1 Tim. 6:17–19).

Why does God give us things so richly? Paul says that it is so we can *enjoy* them. But misers and tight-wads don't enjoy anything, which is why Paul requires the wealthy to be open-handed and liberal in good works, using all that they have and are enjoying. If they do this, they will continue to enjoy their wealth. If they do not, then the cancer sets in.

We see exactly the same thing in Deuteronomy. Notice the *godly* combination of rejoicing in the stuff God has given along with rejoicing in the prospect of sharing it. "And now, behold, I have brought the first-fruits of the land, which thou, O LORD, hast given me. And thou shalt set it before the LORD thy God, and worship before the LORD thy God: And thou shalt rejoice in every good thing which the LORD thy God hath given unto thee, and unto thine house, thou, and the Levite, and the stranger that is among you" (Deut. 26:10–11).

Later in Deuteronomy, God warns the Israelites about the covenant curses. "Because thou servedst not the LORD thy God with joyfulness, and with gladness of heart, *for the abundance of all things*; Therefore shalt thou serve thine enemies which the LORD shall send against thee, in hunger, and in thirst, and in nakedness, and in want of all things: and he shall put a yoke of iron upon thy neck, until he have destroyed thee" (Deut. 28:47–48).

Why did God threaten to expel them from the land? Because they refused to rejoice in all of their stuff. Their idolatry did not consist of having material things. It consisted of being ungrateful for their material things. Again, this is a warning from *Deuteronomy*.

The same God who commanded the Israelites in the fifth chapter of Deuteronomy not to covet is the God who told them they would be expelled from the land because they did not serve God with joy and gladness of heart over the abundance of all the things.

So when it comes to covenant blessings and curses, material prosperity, true heart religion, the idolatry of covetousness, the necessity of radical discipleship, and all the other issues touched on above, there is no appreciable difference between the Old Testament and the New.

And while the phrase "no appreciable difference" sounds pretty tame, the implications are enormous... and glorious. A pietistic gnosticism has been one of our besetting sins. For dedicated Christians, for those who take their faith seriously, the temptation has consistently been to internalize everything. Our faith must begin with the heart, sure enough, but, as I am fond of saying, theology comes out your fingertips. And in addition, whatever is coming out your fingertips, that is your theology.

Christ was God's incarnate gift to us. He took on a human body, thus sanctifying the body. This means that the Christian faith, rightly understood, stands for incarnate realities. We are to live out an incarnate faith, exulting in the things of earth. And why? Because we have set our hearts on things above.

AS OLIVE BRANCHES, WE SHOULD EXTEND AN OLIVE BRANCH

As we have already seen, what happens in the New Covenant is the universalization of Israel, not the annihilation of Israel. Israel is not replaced by this new thing, an entirely different entity called the Christian church. Rather, the priesthood that used to be the prerogative of Jews alone became a priesthood that was opened up to Greeks, Japanese, Scythians, Swedes, and Mayans. The orthodox Christian claim is that the Christian church is now the true Israel of God.

The Jews, naturally, are not persuaded by this. So as we are drawing near to the close of this encouraging line of thought, we still need to raise the practical question: how is the conversion of the Jews to be brought about?

There are two scriptural ways in which this case is to be made to the Jews. We see the first way in many places in the New Testament, which is to resort to the Scriptures. We need to appeal to the law and the prophets.

How did the apostle Paul approach the Jewish leaders in Rome?

> "For this cause therefore have I called for you, to
> see you, and to speak with you: because that *for
> the hope of Israel* I am bound with this chain...."
> And when they had appointed him a day, there
> came many to him into his lodging; to whom he
> expounded and testified the kingdom of God,
> persuading them concerning Jesus, both out of
> the law of Moses, and out of the prophets, from
> morning till evening. (Acts 28:20, 23)

And Paul plainly describes the church as being the Israel of God. "And as many as walk according to this rule, peace be on them, and mercy, and upon the Israel of God" (Gal. 6:16).

All believers in Christ are olive branches that partake of the root and fatness of the Abrahamic tree. And because children of Abraham resort to the law and to the testimony whenever they can, they open their

Bibles in order to reason with the Jews from the text. So that is one way to approach it.

But there is another strategy, a strategy that Paul outlines in Romans 11. There he argues for an incarnational way of making the case. Who has been the heir of all the promises that God made to His people in Deuteronomy? Who is actually walking under those Deuteronomic blessings?

At root, the debate between Christians and Jews has to do with the identity of the true Israel. Who is the true Israel of God? And just as Elijah cried out on Mount Carmel, saying that the God who answered with fire from Heaven was the true God, so it is in this case. The YHWH who dispenses Deuteronomic blessings on His people is thereby identifying who His people actually are. Let the true Jews, the Jews who are Jews inwardly, by the regeneration of the Holy Spirit (Rom. 2:29), be the ones who walk under the grace of all His covenant blessings.

Paul knows His people according to the flesh. He knows that the cultivated branches who have been excised from the olive tree are going to notice it when these rude outsiders, these uncircumcised Philistines, start living in the blessing of Heaven. Paul knows that this is a strategy that will work. The cornucopia of grace trumps all the high intensity accomplishments of striving and high attainment.

CHAPTER 10

American Exceptionalism

THE QUESTION OF AMERICAN EXCEP-
tionalism might seem like an odd thing to include in a
book of this nature, but it really is important—for reasons that should become apparent in just a moment.

I want to argue for a form of American exceptionalism, but it is crucial that we distinguish it from the
much more common articulations of it, expressions
which I consider to be fundamentally idolatrous. And
idolatry never leads to anything good.

The history of the world is a long history of different nations rising to the top of the heap, and during
their time there, rejoicing in whatever form of "exceptionalism" might be on display. We are talking about

Babylonian exceptionalism, Persian exceptionalism, Hellenistic exceptionalism, and Roman exceptionalism, running our gaze from the top of Nebuchadnezzar's statue to the very bottom. Many empires have had their day in the sun, and during the time of their hegemony, they were pleased to believe what their sages told them, which was "we're number one."

This applies to more empires than those that made it into Nebuchadnezzar's statue—it includes the Sumerians, the Assyrians, the Ottomans, the British, and the Americans. America is now the world's hegemon, and what else is new? There's always somebody.

The popular expressions of American exceptionalism are as old as dirt. There is nothing new about top dogs vaunting themselves over their top dogginess. This is the most unexceptional form of exceptionalism possible. This high school has been here for many decades, and nobody currently knows who the senior class president was twenty-five years ago. Nobody knows because nobody cares.

But there are two ways in which America really has been exceptional. I want to introduce both of those elements now because they will be fitted into the larger argument later.

The first exceptional thing about America is that the men who founded it knew we were not exceptional. They budgeted for our ordinariness. They anticipated the possible failures and corruptions that would beset us, and did a remarkable job with the constitutional structures they instituted.

If you were from another planet, and someone gave you a mastery of English and a copy of the U.S. Constitution, there is one fundamental takeaway from that Constitution that should be glaring and obvious: never, ever trust an American, especially Americans who hold political office.

The whole thing is structured in such a way as to not rely on the good faith of our leaders. The fact that such good faith could evaporate is taken for granted. Our distrust of them is seen in how our apparatus of government takes advantage of the rulers' distrust of one another.

Our system of checks and balances is pretty intricate. At the federal level, we have three branches of government—the executive, the legislative, and the judicial. The legislative branch is itself divided into two chambers, the Senate and the House, with the House designed to respond to the people directly, and the Senate designed to respond to the interests of the states. The same kind of checks and balances exist on the state level—with executive, legislative, and judicial branches. And on top of that, the authority of the central government and the state governments are put in tension as well.

All of this is to prevent too much political power from accumulating in one place. And this is because the Founders knew, as Lord Acton later expressed it, that power corrupts, and absolute power corrupts absolutely. The Founders did not establish this Constitution to protect future generations from the British. We already had our independence from Britain. They did all this to protect future generations of Americans from Americans.

They did this because they knew that Americans are nothing special. They knew that Americans were not exceptional—and knowing that really was exceptional. Lincoln told us that we were dedicated to the proposition that all men are created equal, but there was another proposition just as relevant, which is that all men are equally *fallen*.

This is why Madison said in *Federalist* 51, "In framing a government which is to be administered by men over men, the great difficulty lies in this: You must first enable the government to control the governed; and in the next place, oblige it to control itself."

Knowing this, and budgeting for the reality that when it comes to power, all men are alcoholics, and that unlimited and unrestrained power is a large bottle of 100 proof *Dead Carrion Reserve*, our Founders were truly exceptional.

The distressing fact is that many ostensible conservatives have succumbed to the "national greatness" line, and talk about American exceptionalism in the "old as dirt" way of talking about it. But this is how

Nebuchadnezzar was thinking right before his bovine period. "The king spake, and said, Is not this great Babylon, that I have built for the house of the kingdom by the might of my power, and for the honour of my majesty?" (Dan. 4:30).

When men think and talk like this, puffing themselves up, they are on the threshold of lunacy. All I can think about is the head of the Statue of Liberty, surrounded by miles of lone and level sands. And because it is America, maybe some tumbleweed.

> My name is Ozymandias, King of Kings;
> Look on my Works, ye Mighty, and despair!
> Nothing beside remains. Round the decay
> Of that colossal Wreck, boundless and bare
> The lone and level sands stretch far away.

It is unique among men to know that you are nothing much. It is a humdrum thing to think of yourself as unique and very special. Because we have been rapidly losing the Christian moorings of our understanding of law and politics, we are becoming quite ordinary.

AMERICAN POWERBALL

But there is another sense in which America has been exceptional, and this one has to be handled with great care also. America has been exceptionally blessed; we were given a land flowing with milk and honey. Given what we were given, we should feel like the winners of American Powerball.

This abundance fed into a particular narrative that we took for granted, and so we have to untie a few knots.

When a Christian nation has a period of hegemonic ascendency—as has happened multiple times—it's the easiest thing in the world to drift into a mistaken conflation of material prosperity and special cove-nantal status. But no nation of Christendom will ever occupy the same place or position that Israel did. This is because the church—which is international in its genius—was commanded to disciple all of the nations, not leaving any of them out. So there will never be a Christian nation that will be *the* chosen nation. That is no longer an option.

Americans have long thought of themselves as being set apart. Abraham Lincoln once spoke of Americans as an "almost chosen" people. In *White Jacket*, Herman Melville said this: "We Americans are the peculiar, chosen people—the Israel of our time; we bear the ark of the liberties of the world."[1] This has been going on for a very long time. In the seventeenth century, John Winthrop used the phrase "city on a hill," taken from Matthew's gospel, in order to describe the new American commonwealth. The

1. Herman Melville, *White Jacket* (London: Richard Bentley, 1850), 238–239.

phrase has been extraordinarily sticky, down to the time of Ronald Reagan.

One of the key elements in the Puritan project of New England was at just this point. George McKenna summarizes the Puritan Americans' sense of mission very well: "America as ancient Israel. America's historical role parallels that of ancient Israel: Americans are God's special people, sent into a desert wilderness to carry out a divine 'errand' there and set an example for the world."[2]

At the beginning this was grounded in Scripture, and in a peculiar kind of postmillennial vision. No less a worthy than Jonathan Edwards was affected by it. This initial version of the vision was Bible-believing, and so it was that a sense of destiny and mission, with a lot of territory to the west just sitting there, got down into the American DNA. Gradually the robust connection of all this to the gospel began to wane, but the optimism remained. It still shows up in the foreign policies of men like Woodrow Wilson and George W. Bush. The idea of America as messiah-nation is an idea that dies hard, but die it must.

But with that said, in the providence of God, America obviously has *some* purpose in God's plan. We can say this because absolutely everything has a purpose in God's plan, and so to confess this is not putting on airs. The word "chosen" can be used in lesser senses.

2. George McKenna, *The Puritan Origins of American Patriotism* (New Haven, CT: Yale University Press, 2007), 49.

Armenia was probably the first nation to confess Christ, and so they were chosen for that. Britain used her military prowess at sea to suppress the slave trade, and so she was chosen for that. In order to try to figure out what America's purpose might be, while staying far away from the hubris of thinking of ourselves as some kind of new Israel, we have to look steadily at what sorts of things have been given to us. And with that, I will appear to be changing the subject, but I am not really doing so.

I live in northern Idaho, up in the panhandle. About thirty miles south of us is the town of Lewiston, Idaho, right at the confluence of the Snake River and the Clearwater. I bring this up because Lewiston is a seven-hour drive from the Pacific Ocean, and is what might be described as "way inland." And yet, Lewiston is a *seaport*. Farmers in our area can make a short drive there, and ship their crop anywhere in the world.

I mention this for several reasons. One is that shipping by water is far more inexpensive than other means of transport—geopoliticist Peter Zeihan puts the practical ratio anywhere from 40:1 to 70:1.[3] Now the United States has about 17,000 miles of navigable rivers, which is more than the rest of the world combined.[4] And what's more, three of those major rivers, the Mississippi, the Missouri, and the Ohio,

3. Peter Zeihan, *The Accidental Superpower* (New York: Twelve, 2014), 12.
4. Ibid., 46–47.

are plonked right on top of one of the largest pieces of arable land in the world, the great middle section of America, where we grow enough corn to make ancient Joseph's eyes bulge. All this, taken together, means that the average American farmer is within a short drive of getting an abundant crop shipped cheaply. Given the geographical layout of our nation, we would have had to work very hard to be poor.

I am going to give a few more reasons for this in a minute, but I do need to introduce one qualifier. I have learned a great deal about this topic from Peter Zeihan, and have been most grateful to him for all of it. But the one thing he tends to background or minimize is the faith or the worldview of the people who inhabit different regions of the world. He is almost a geographical determinist, and this leaves out what George Gilder so helpfully emphasizes—the people, and the way those people think and behave. And the people are going to be shaped and directed by their worldview. North America had all the resources I am describing long before Columbus landed, and yet the inhabitants didn't utilize them the same way they were used later.

When it comes to natural resources, Venezuela was one of the richest countries in South America, and the curse of envy-ridden socialism absolutely wrecked them. In the mid-twentieth century, one of the richest cities in the southern part of our hemisphere was Havana, and one of the richest cities in the northern part was Detroit. When it comes to wrecking the blessings of God, human stupidity is certainly up to the challenge.

So I am here pointing out some of the key natural advantages that Americans have been blessed with, which means that we really would have to work hard to be poor. But if we don't count out that can-do American spirit, and if we elect just a few more commies, then we should be able to get there.

Back to our advantages. This land of natural abundance is highly defensible. We have two oceanic moats on either side of us—in order to be invaded from east or west, it would require a huge naval power. But *we* are that huge naval power. We are a maritime people, and have been from the beginning. By virtually every metric, the US Navy is the most powerful in the world.[5]

To the north we have thinly populated Canada, and most of that population lives within a hundred miles of the US-Canada border. From that direction we can detect massive amounts of annoyance, but no military threat. Mexico, despite the immigration problems we are currently having, is not really a military threat either.

Up and down our Atlantic and Pacific coasts we have an astounding number of natural harbors. Ease of access for trade is the greatest of blessings, while

5. Sinéad Baker, "The world's most powerful navies in 2023, ranked," *Insider*, 6 August 2023, https://www.businessinsider.com/most-powerful-navies-in-world-in-2023-ranked-ships-submarines-2023-8.

difficulty of access for military purposes is also among the greatest of blessings.

Then there is the energy question. We have enough energy in the ground, already discovered, to meet our current energy needs for centuries to come. It is cheerfully granted that environmentalists have told you differently, but it should also be cheerfully noted that environmentalists are notorious liars.

I mentioned the worldview of the people earlier, and here is where a potent combination took shape historically. This continent was settled by people who were the very embodiment of the Puritan work ethic. It was truly a land of milk and honey. With a resource-rich continent as a head start, with its millions of square miles of green clover, an industrious swarm of Calvinist bees set about making more honey than the world had ever imagined possible. And armies of Dutch dairy farmers thought we needed oceans of milk, American scale.

Many years ago, a British gent was visiting our community, and someone took him to Costco. After he saw a fifty-pound sack of almonds there, he said that he saw no conceivable use for them, and yet, he said, he felt "strangely drawn."

It is hard to comprehend just how wealthy America is. We can take this in a bit more fully if we compare the GDP of various American *cities* to that of other *countries*. For just a handful of examples, taken from many, the New York metro area produces as much as all of Canada. The Miami area is step-for-step with Israel. The Houston area competes with Chile, Los Angeles with Malaysia, and Seattle with Ukraine.[6] This is, speaking quite frankly, and just between us girls, ridiculous.

We still need to place this in the context of the larger argument, which will happen shortly. In the meantime, we should heed the words of Deuteronomy. Deuteronomy keeps coming up somehow.

> And it shall be, when the LORD thy God shall have brought thee into the land which he sware unto thy fathers, to Abraham, to Isaac, and to Jacob, to give thee great and goodly cities, which thou buildedst not, And houses full of all good things, which thou filledst not, and wells digged, which thou diggedst not, vineyards and olive trees, which thou plant- edst not; when thou shalt have eaten and be full; Then beware lest thou forget the LORD, which brought thee forth out of the land of Egypt, from the house of bondage. (Deut. 6:10–12)

All of our blessings should have been an occasion for great gratitude and humility, but as is so often

---

6. Juan Carlos, "Visualizing 20 American Cities with Economies as Big as Countries," howmuch.net, 25 February 2020, https://howmuch.net /articles/economic-output-largest-us-metro-areas-compared-countries.

the case in such circumstances, Jeshurun waxed fat and kicked. As Cotton Mather once put it, faithfulness begat prosperity, and the daughter devoured the mother. We were given a multitude of rivers, rich soil for agriculture, defensible borders, spacious harbors, enormous amounts of energy in the ground, and quite a bit more than that. But it is always difficult to keep money from doing what money always does (Deut. 8:10–14).

As Jesus reminds us in Luke 12, to whom much is given, much is required. In our American ingratitude, we are looking to become the servant of verse 47, the one who will be beaten with many stripes. The only appropriate response to enormous material blessings is humility and gratitude. We have responded with the precise opposite—conceit and ingratitude. We have thought that a lush and productive land is somehow our birthright, guaranteed to us in the Bill of Rights. We call it the American Dream.

Apart from faith in God, apart from the forgiveness of Christ, such blessings only tantalize what might be called the American Daydream. To have a multitude of natural blessings alone is not really a blessing. The more green and lush it is in the rainy season, the more there is to burn in the dry.

In the missionary hymn "From Greenland's Icy Mountains," the former bishop of Calcutta referred to the fact that a place can be greatly blessed in one way, and fall grievously short in another—where "every prospect pleases, and only man is vile."

"And Lot lifted up his eyes, and beheld all the plain of Jordan, that it was well watered every where, before the LORD destroyed Sodom and Gomorrah, even as the garden of the LORD, like the land of Egypt, as thou comest unto Zoar" (Gen. 13:10). Oooo! Let's move there. I hear the Cities of the Plain are exceptional.

We in America have been extraordinarily blessed. We have also, commensurate with that, been extraordinarily ungrateful.

AMERICAN ZIONISM AND THE CREED

Ancient Israel really did have the promises and the covenants. God really had spoken to them from Sinai, and really had set them apart as a peculiar people. If it was possible for them to sin impudently by taking it all for granted, how much greater the impudence for a people who did not have such unique promises to start acting as though we had? This is the position that America is in today.

The coming salvation of the Jews means salvation for the world, and this salvation for the Jews will come when enough Gentile nations start laying claim to the Deuteronomic blessings. This will provoke the Jews to jealousy, and when they return to their Messiah, what will this mean but an enormous blessing for the world? For many reasons, grounded in the unmerited kindness of God, the United States has been in a perfect position to live out what it means for Gentiles to rejoice under such Deuteronomic blessings. But despite our roaring start, and a really good run, we have fallen into the trap of envious sin, as expressed in our soulless and secular liberalism, with the inevitable growth of antisemitism.

How did we get here?

One important clue can be seen in how David Gelernter really celebrates the Puritans: "To understand America and Americanism, you must understand those Puritans. They are a difficult proposition, an intellectual handful. They were religious fanatics. But their intolerance gave birth to toleration; their quest for religious freedom yielded freedom in general; and their devotion to the Bible and the biblical idea of covenant contributed significantly to the modern liberal state." [7]

Now, before I get into everything I agree with Gelernter about, I need to note one point of drastic disagreement. The Puritans *did* in fact shape the American personality. But personality is not the same thing as character. Two men can have an outgoing personality, with one of them honest and the other treacherous. Two men can be quiet and withdrawn,

---

7. David Gelerntner, *Americanism: The Fourth Great Western Religion* (New York: Doubleday, 2007), 38.

with one of them a rock of integrity and the other a knave. We do share certain personality features with the Puritans, attributes we inherited from them. But inheriting their personality is not the same thing as inheriting their character.

To hear praise of the Puritans like this is like hearing the Prodigal Son raise a toast in some seedy tavern (Distant Country Ale House) in honor of his father, who supplied him with all this *great* money. Just like in the parable, there will come a day when we run out of all that "great money" that the Puritans supplied us with. We may actually already be there—the pig food is starting to look pretty good.

But still, Gelernter is onto something. In his argument, Gelernter gives us a short course in the history of Protestant Calvinism, and points out some helpful connections. For example, why has America been relatively free from certain viral attitudes that have afflicted Christendom in old Europe? "Calvin's influence also paved the way for English and (even more) American affection for the Old Testament; for English and (far more) American resistance to antisemitism."[8]

Some wit once said that Scots Presbyterianism was "pork-eating Judaism," and the Scots and Scotch-Irish who streamed to the New World in the eighteenth century supplemented the Puritan affection for "Old

8. Gelerntner, *Americanism*, 45.

Testament Christianity." Americans have historically been biblicists, and they have included both testaments in their biblicism. Look at all the American place names that line up with Old Testament towns and cities: Salem, Bethlehem, Philadelphia, Rehoboth, Smyrna, Hebron, Gilead, Nazareth, and many more. Even Newark is a shortened form of New Ark of the Covenant. And then consider how many men in nineteenth-century America were named Obadiah.

Gelernter also points to specific characteristics of the Puritans that contributed greatly to the American personality. The most striking is the emphasis on *simplicity*. "Simplicity as a worldview was especially important in America. Reinforced by the natural limitations of New World life far from European craftsmen, models, and materials, restrained simplicity emerged as *the* American style—an aesthetic with theological roots."[9]

This passion for simplicity brought a fatal temptation with it. It is one of the reasons for the precipitous fall of New England Puritanism into Unitarianism in the nineteenth century. The Trinity is more complicated than the "simplicity" of Unitarianism. Gelernter sees this decline, but has an odd response to it. "When the bright blaze of Puritanism was replaced by the pale flicker of Unitarianism, a spiritual vacuum appeared

9. Gelerntner, *Americanism*, 54.

on the American landscape. Eventually it was replaced by Americanism itself. The American Religion was the true heir of Puritanism."[10]

What he doesn't see is that, biblically speaking, his Americanism is just another pale flicker, a candle guttering in front of yet another idol. The solitary monad god of the Unitarians was an idol—one that not very many people wanted to worship because doing so unfortunately involved spending time with Unitarians. And the solitary monad god of American civil religion, the one currently invoked on our money and in our pledge of allegiance, *is in principle the same kind of idol*. But *this* idol is a lot sexier, and has a lot more enthusiastic (camp) followers, mostly because the American economy churns out goods and services in a vast torrent, and we mustn't leave out American military firepower and throw-weight. Chicks dig an armed guy in uniform with lots of cash. The prophet Ezekiel describes a very similar fascination that the "Chaldeans in vermilion" managed to create in *their* day: "For she doted upon their paramours, whose flesh is as the flesh of asses, and whose issue is like the issue of horses" (Ezek. 23:20). Nothing succeeds like success, and power and wealth are sexy enough to turn weak heads. Americanism is therefore an idolatry that appears to have a lot going for it. But Christians who

10. Gelerntner, *Americanism*, 56.

worship the triune God will refuse to worship *any* idol, whether it is the nerdy monad of the liberal bedwetters, or the gonad monad of the American neocons.

Gelernter says that Americanism consists "of American Zionism and the Creed."[11] I would add that American Zionism is postmillennial wine turned to vinegar, and the Creed is a bastardized attempt to apply certain blessings found only in Christ to a civil order outside of Christ, a civil order which *rejects* Christ.

First, the Zionism. The Puritans thought of themselves as a new chosen people, settling into a new promised land. They held this in the context of a postmillennial vision of the gospel extending to the ends of the earth. This Zionistic impulse is why Americans tend to think that events on the other side of the world are somehow our business, and if our business, then shortly thereafter the business of the American military. The Church believes this rightly, because Christ told us to take the gospel to all nations. But secularize the doctrine and you have Woodrow Wilson's foreign policy, which incidentally has been the foreign policy of virtually *all* modern presidents. If you want to know what postmillennialism looks like with Jesus taken out of it, look no further than George Bush's Second Inaugural. This is an example of us taking the promise for granted, and it is worse

11. Gelerntner, *Americanism*, 57.

than what ancient Israel did because we were never actually given such a unique promise. We were given staggering *gifts* which we assumed were a promise, and then took all of it for granted.

The Creed, as Gelernter presents it, is "liberty, equality, democracy."[12] But if this is being presented to us as a series of answers to basic religious questions, we need to be prepared for the follow-up questions. Why should men be free? Why should they be treated with equity? Why should we govern ourselves democratically? The answers will vary depending on whether you believe that we evolved out of the primordial goo, or whether the Creator God, the Father of the Lord Jesus Christ, put us here. They will vary according to whether you believe in the Supreme Court or the Supreme Being.

Religions don't do well suspended in mid-air. Why should men be free? Who makes them free? How can they be free when they are slaves to sin?

If an Americanist evangelist shows up at your door with free literature (perhaps around election time), I would suggest raising such questions and pressing them home. "Why should we fight for liberty? Why should we care?" The apologist for any new religion will have to do better than, "Three hundred and fifty years ago there were some people on the East Coast

12. Gelerntner, *Americanism*, 69.

who used to believe in God and His Son, Jesus Christ. We don't anymore, of course, but they really inspire us with their upbeat, can-do attitude."

It reminds me of the old joke about the apostle Paul, apostle of depravity and sovereign grace, and Norman Vincent Peale, apostle of Uplift. A fellow was asked to compare them and he said, "I find Paul appealing, and Peale appalling." Paul is *profound*, and consequently overflowing with good news, while those who heal the wound of the people lightly will always be merely dabbing around the festering edges. Deriving shallow inspiration from those who used to believe something deeply is just that—*shallow*. You cannot have it both ways.

The way out is repentance. The only solution to the dire situation we find ourselves in now is reformation and revival. We refused, for various reasons, to walk in a manner that was worthy of the kindness we had received. That being the case, the remaining question has to be, "How can we get back on track?"

CHAPTER 11

American Milk and Honey

UP TO THIS POINT, THIS BOOK HAS resembled a jumbled box of different colored tiles. This last chapter is the place where you are supposed to be able to see the mosaic. Let us shake hands all around and wish each other luck.

God's plan has always been the salvation of the entire world. His purpose has always included all the nations of men. In the very first book of the Bible, He promised Abraham that he would be the instrument of blessing for all the families of the earth (Gen. 12:3). We are not out of line, therefore, if we look downstream in history to see what happens to all the families of the earth.

Toward this end, Jehovah called and set aside the nation of Israel. There were many reasons for this, but two of the main reasons were, first, to cultivate a people from whom the Messiah would arise, and second, to demonstrate the lessons He had prepared for all the nations by summoning one nation up to the front of class. When Israel did well, the other nations could see how the God of Heaven was willing to bless the sons of men—as the Queen of Sheba could well testify. But when the chosen nation forgot the Lord and turned aside to idols, the Lord would judge them severely, such that everyone who heard of it would find their ears tingling.

So Israel was not the *saved* nation, but rather the representative nation, the priestly nation. What was given to them was given so that other nations could look to them and learn. The lessons learned might be cautionary, and they might be exemplary.

And so, after centuries of preparation, the Messiah finally came. He was rejected by the chief priests and scribes, and in a travesty of justice, executed—just like so many other prophets before him. But this time something went desperately wrong, at least from the perspective of the Establishment Men. This time, the executed prophet did something no one else had been able to do: come back from the dead. This made Him very difficult to deal with. Now He is ruling from the right hand of the Father, and is entirely out of their reach.

The leaders of the Jews had Christ executed, as Pilate saw, out of envy (Matt. 27:18). This means envy was the iniquity that resulted in the savage judgment that fell on Jerusalem in AD 70. And then, under a man named Bar Kochba, a second revolt against Rome occurred about half a century after the AD 70 revolt. When this second revolt was crushed, the Jews were exiled from the land, and as a consequence, scattered everywhere.

Since then, the Jews have been in something of a permanent exile. The Babylonian exile at the time of Jeremiah was merely 70 years. This latest dispersion has to date been thousands of years. And even today with the restoration of Israel as a nation, the number of Jews outside Israel exceeds the number within Israel. If we use the metric that Israel uses—the "Law of Return" under which a person is eligible for Israeli citizenship— there are around 25 million Jews in the world. About 53 percent of these are in the United States, and 27 percent in Israel. The rest are spread across countries including France, Germany, Canada, the UK, and Brazil.[1] The bulk of the Jewish population worldwide remains a stranger in a strange land. And even in Israel, a secular state, where devout Jews are influential in Israeli politics, they still occupy the margins.

1. Sergio DellaPergolla, "World Jewish Population, 2021," in *American Jewish Year Book 2021*, eds. Arnold Dashefsky and Ira M. Sheskin (Springer, 2022), 313-412.

While the Jews were out wandering the wilderness, Christians everywhere were establishing and growing Christendom. In principle, this meant that various Christian nations had access to the promises of Deuteronomy, and in varying degrees enjoyed them. We see some examples in France, Germany, the UK, and the Netherlands. But the country where it has been preeminently true has been the United States.

As was made clear earlier in this book, there is not any nonsense here about a chosen nation, or some kind of genetic American exceptionalism. We are not talking about any explicit promises in Scripture concerning America, as some people dream. But Scripture does contain promises about the providential course of the gospel down through history, a providential course that certainly includes us, and so we may be excused for having eyes in our heads.

The logic of Christendom is that of multiple countries, multiple nations, all calling on the name of Christ, all having the option of living under the promised Deuteronomic blessings. As this goodness gradually takes shape, these Deuteronomic blessings will gradually become the Isaianic blessings, and the wolf shall dwell with the lamb.

Now in the providence of God, a number of striking things came together in the Founding of the United States. They were, in order, the first settlements coming from historically Protestant countries, with the settlers by and large pious and devout. The second thing was that the land in the middle swath of North America was indeed a land flowing with milk and honey—the soil, the rivers, the mines, the forests, and the climate. The third thing was that the two immense oceans on either side of America formed a giant moat that made the Monroe Doctrine a feasible option.

If ever there was any nation poised to beta test the apostle Paul's strategy, it was the United States. And there have been stretches of time where it was possible to see it taking shape. Our nation has historically been an exuberant cascading torrent of Protestant Gentiles doing lots of cool stuff, from skyscrapers, to telephones, to assembly lines, to landing on the moon. We have been in love with what one writer called the "technological sublime." And yes, I know there are loyal Americans who are Catholics, Jews, and so on, which means that I know I am generalizing. Work with me. In fact, most of the Jews in the world are here, watching everything we do, up close and personal.

There is one more striking thing about this whole set up: America is the first nation to have such a large population of Jews that has also not had an egregious problem with antisemitism. Yes, that mental disease has existed here, but nothing like it has in Europe. Generally speaking, Americans have been remarkably free of the fuel that causes antisemitism to burn really hot, and, as already argued, that fuel is envy.

Americans have not been threatened by this "high performance people" largely because Americans have historically been a high performance people themselves. We appreciate and like the competition.

But as identity politics and socialist envy rot out our institutions, particularly our education system, the average American graduate is joining the swelling ranks of what might be called "low performance people." And not only are they low performance people, they are low performance people who have been flattered their entire lives, and who consequently feel pretty entitled. And if there is one thing that such people know how to do, it is to envy.

In the death of Christ, we see the crucifixion of all envy in principle. When Christ died, the dragon of envy was impaled there on His cross, like the serpent in the wilderness. So one of the first lessons that every Christian should learn is the virtue of hating envy. This is a lesson that American Christians must relearn. We knew it once, but we must come back to this point in a spirit of humility.

Remember the parable of *Chariots of Fire*. In that movie, both Harold Abrahams and Eric Liddell are great athletes. They both earn their medal in the Olympics. But Harold Abrahams, the Jew, runs under the law, while Eric Liddell, the Christian, runs under the pleasure of God. The Jews still run like Harold Abrahams. Americans used to run like Eric Liddell. Let the reader understand.

America is currently engaged in a large-scale attempt to forget the God who blessed us, and as that happens, *mutatis mutandis*, the curses of Ebal will apply to us, just as the blessings of Gerazim once rested on us.

We should continue to pray and labor for reformation and revival in America not just to avoid spiraling into the chaos of missed opportunities, but to get back on track, and be used by God to reach the Jews. When the Jews come back to their rejected Christ, that will be glory for the world.

If we repent and learn to seek first the kingdom, Jesus says that "all these things will be added." If we selfishly seek to cling to those things apart from loyalty to the one who gives them, we are like a miser in a shipwreck who holds tightly to his two bags of gold, weights that take him straight to the bottom.

The future as I am envisioning it rides on reformation and revival among American Christians. We should be asking God to give us what only He can give us. But as we pray, we should remember two things. The first is that God has promised that the world will in fact be blessed in this way. The second is that for us to be a part of this blessing, the only thing necessary would be for God to nod His head.

APPENDIX 1
A Glossary

AT A DECEMBER 1, 2022, MEETING OF Knox Presbytery (Communion of Reformed Evangelical Churches), we adopted a short statement on a particular form of ethnic sin. That statement summarized a central theme of this book, and so we will begin there.

On Antisemitism
We believe the conversion of the Jews is key to the success of Christ's Great Commission, and it is incumbent upon us to pray and labor toward that end. While, apart from Christ, the Jews are as all others—alienated from God—they have remained

an object of God's care because the gifts and calling of God are irrevocable. God's plan for converting them is for them to see Gentile nations under the blessings of Christ's lordship, thus leading them to long for the same. Hence, the cancerous sin of antisemitism has no place in God's plan.

So then, to the glossary.

This glossary is arranged in alphabetical order, so if you want to make any systematic sense of it, you may have to read through it twice. And some of the definitions and explanations will overlap. This is not meant to irritate you, but rather to enrich your experience, and you are most welcome.

Abrahamic Faiths

This is a common way of referring to Christianity, Judaism, and Islam, as though the fact that we are all "people of the book" minimizes the differences between us. While it is true that there are numerous historical connections, and a shared history at many points, this could also be said of Israel, Edom, Ammon, and Moab. The fact that we all have a book doesn't mean that the books say the same things.

Antisemitism

Antisemitism is the notion that Jews are uniquely malevolent and destructive in their cultural, economic, and political influence in the world. As defined elsewhere, ethnic sin is either malicious, vainglorious, or separatist (with the desire for separation driven by either malice or vainglory), but the antisemitic forms of it usually tend toward the malicious. It is not antisemitism to believe that Jews are sinful. This is simply orthodox Christianity. All of us are sinful. But antisemitism does believe that Jews are *uniquely* sinful, and particularly destructive. As a stand-alone dogma, this is nonsense. What plausibility it has in the minds of some can be accounted for under the entry below entitled "High Performance People."

Ashkenazi Jews

Jews worldwide can be divided into three major groupings. There are the Middle Eastern Jews, Sephardic Jews (Spain, Portugal), and Ashkenazi Jews (Central and Eastern Europe). A common assertion among antisemites is that the Ashkenazi Jews converted to Judaism a number of centuries after Christ, and thus there is not a drop of Abraham's blood in their veins. This matters to them because over 90 percent of American Jews are Ashkenazi and around 50 percent of Israeli Jews are. A lot of what we identify as Jewish is actually Yiddish (Ashkenazi). However, it doesn't really matter if the Ashkenazi are all descended from some Turkic tribe that converted to Judaism centuries ago. When Abraham was circumcised, his whole household (with hundreds of men in it, including his slaves) were also circumcised (Gen. 17:23). This means that a bunch of the first generation Jews—plank owners—did not have Abraham's DNA in them either. It has always been a matter of covenant, not blood. So for Christians what this question should amount to is whether a tribe of people could bind themselves by covenant to the line of Hagar (Gal. 4:25). And the answer is *yes*.

Biblical Scholarship

The fact that Jews do not accept that Jesus was their Messiah has not robbed them of their ability to contribute significantly to biblical scholarship. From the time of the Reformation on, Christians have been noted for their willingness to learn particular things from the rabbis, including Hebrew. The fact that scholars (like Robert Alter) do not see their Christ in the text does not mean they see nothing in the text.

Christian

In all these discussions, I use the word *Christian* in two senses. The first refers to someone who accepts the truth of the Apostles' Creed, and who has been baptized in the triune name. This means that the individual concerned is not a Buddhist, Hindu, Muslim, etc. The second use of the word *Christian* refers to someone who has the root of the matter in him, and who has been born again to new life in Christ. This means that the individual concerned is not going to Hell when he dies.

Claims of the Messiah

Jesus is either the Messiah promised in the Old Testament, or He is not. There is no real way to split the difference on such a question. If the claim is false, then Christians are guilty of perpetuating the most preposterous fraud ever. If the claim is true, then pious Jews studying the Old Testament are like Shakespeare scholars who have devoted their lives to the study of Hamlet, but who have failed to recognize the prince of Denmark. As just mentioned, it is not possible to have Jesus be the Messiah "for the Christians" and not the Messiah "for the Jews." That might seem a mild form of relativism, but relativism always metastasizes.

Conversion of the Jews

In classical Reformation theology, the conversion of the Jews was the long hoped-for, long prayed-for event that was to usher in the evangelization of the entire world. Andrew Marvell refers to it in his poem about his coy mistress, and the Westminster divines included it in their Larger Catechism. Question 191 asks what we pray for when we pray for the kingdom to come. Among other things, we pray for "the gospel [to be] propagated throughout the world, the Jews called, [and] the fulness of the Gentiles brought in." This was held because of their broadly shared interpretation of Romans 11, see below.

Covenant

A covenant is a solemn bond, sovereignly administered, with attendant blessings and curses. This is the structure of all covenants, including the covenants that bind people in their unbelief. The apostle Paul teaches that unbelieving Jews are in covenant with Hagar, not Sarah (Gal. 4:25), and that whenever Moses is read, a veil lies over their heart (2 Cor. 3:15).

Cultural Disintegration

When previously stable societies start to disintegrate, as ours is currently doing, it is easy for distressed individuals to start looking for easy answers, and readily identifiable scapegoats. When such a situation arises, hostility to the Jews frequently presents itself as a viable option. For Christians, it is not.

Deuteronomic Blessings

The apostle Paul taught that the blessings to an obedient Israel in Deuteronomy are promises that are available to Gentiles through Christ (Eph. 6:2). This reality is the hinge upon which his argument in Romans 11 turns.

Deuteronomic Strategy

The apostle Paul wants the Gentiles to live under the Deuteronomic blessing of God's covenant kindness. This will result in high achievement by grace, as opposed to the high achievement by dint of raw human effort. The pattern for this is the great contrast set up in the magnificent movie *Chariots of Fire*. There the Jewish runner, Harold Abrahams, is a wonderful runner, but he is under the law. He is driven, and eaten up with ambition. His counterpart, Eric Liddell, the Christian, is also fast, but not driven—rather carried. When he runs, he feels "His pleasure." The structure of this great film sums up everything I want to argue in this book. High achievement *by grace* is something that would provoke the Jews under the law to envy. Paul *wants* to provoke them to envy—Paul knows his people. He knows that this is a people upon whom this strategy will work. Living under Deuteronomic blessing is not a matter of merit, but rather is all of grace. Because it is *gift*, this makes it all look so easy. In contrast to this, the anti-semite envies the Jew and resents his success. This is not antisemitic so much as it is anti-Pauline—and at the end of the day, anti-gospel. So the Jews must be brought to envy us, not the other way around. And the only way this will happen is by grace, only by sovereign grace.

Dispensationalism

It is recognized that there are various strains of dispensationalism, and that what is said here does not apply to all of them. But a common form of dispensationalism holds that God has two peoples, Jews and Christians, and that when the Jews rebuild the Temple

in Jerusalem, animal sacrifices will resume there, and
God will *receive* those sacrifices, the book of Hebrews
notwithstanding. The net result of this theology has
been a form of Christian Zionism—and see "Zionism"
below. Under the Z's.

Egalitarianism
Egalitarianism is a leveling impulse, and egalitarians
resent anyone who through hard work, grit, perseverance, and talent makes them feel small and insignificant. See the next entry on envy.

Envy
Because the Jews are a high-achieving people, they
have a tendency to awaken envy among those who
feel left behind or excluded. Tension between ethnic
groups is frequently a *competitive* tension, and this
should always be remembered.

Ethnic Sin
The modern secular world has made racism the ultimate sin, but it is a sin against *their* catalog of sins. The
Scriptures do not teach us to group people by skin color—
whether to praise or to blame. The Bible *does* teach us
quite a bit about tribes, languages, empires, peoples, and
more, and the theme of this teaching is that in Christ all
such distinctions are backgrounded—but backgrounded
does not mean annihilated or vaporized. As Christians

interact with people from ethnic groupings distinct from theirs, they must not give way to animosity, or to patronizing vainglory, or to separatist avoidance.

Gospel
The gospel is the message that through Christ—through His sinless life, His death, burial, and resurrection—Israel finally got it right. Because of Christ, and through faith in Him, the incident with the golden calf can be forgotten forever.

High Performance People
For many reasons, too variegated to go into here, the Jews are a high performance people. This means that when they are bad, they are high-performance bad. And when they are productive contributing members of society, they are high-performance fruitful and good. Antisemites frequently point to the high preponderance of Jews among the Bolsheviks, say, or pornographers, or the Frankfurt School. What they don't do is point to the counterpart phenomenon when we are talking about violin masters, or patent holders, or Nobel Prize winners, or members of the Austrian School of economics.

Holocaust Denial
In talking about the Holocaust, we need to be careful to define terms. Our language has been so corrupted that we now take any form of disagreement as a denial of

"undisputed" facts. Thus, we now have climate denial, and election denial, and so forth. If a historian decided, after exhaustive research, that the number of Jews who were murdered in the Holocaust was actually closer to 4.9 million than to 6 million, he would be risking his livelihood and career because of how easy it would be for him to be tagged as a Holocaust denier. But he is denying nothing, just disagreeing with others about the math. So I want to reserve the phrase "Holocaust denier" for someone who just flat claims that the entire thing was a Russian slander on the German people, that there was no "final solution," and that the stories about the gas chambers were greatly exaggerated.

Jew

A Jew is someone who has a shared ethnic and cultural heritage with other Jews, going back to the time of Abraham. Proselytes have been grafted in during that time, but as mentioned above, this does not alter the covenantal connection. With this as their shared experience, Jews differ widely among themselves with regard to what they believe—there are secular Jews, Reformed Jews, Conservative Jews, and Orthodox Jews. Not to mention others.

Jewish Humor

One of the things that makes antisemitism such a difficult thing for me to understand is that I so appreciate the distinctive Jewish sense of humor. Okay, hands up, this is not my strongest argument, but I am still going to include it anyhow. One time, shortly before Hitler took power, one of his brown shirts was walking down the street and went past a Jew going the other way. As they passed, the brown shirt sneered and said aloud, "*Schwein.*" The Jew just tipped his hat and said, "Cohen."

Jews and Galileans

Within the pages of the New Testament, a clear distinction is made between two kinds of Jews—Galileans and Judeans. But the Greek word *Ioudaios* can be translated as either "Jew" or "Judean." Given the way the New Testament highlights the differences between the two regions, I think it makes sense to render a number of the passages that are usually translated as "the Jews" differently. Thus: "And therefore did the Judeans persecute Jesus, and sought to slay him, because he had done these things on the sabbath day" (John 5:16).

Judeo-Christian Tradition

I believe that this phrase is inaccurate at worst, and anachronistic at best. The Judeo part of the tradition comes from the fact that Christians never abandoned the Old Testament the way Marcion wanted them to. There is therefore commonality between the Jewish tradition and the Christian tradition, but not a great deal of commonality. Not so much that we could call it one tradition. Again, the place of Jesus is not a detail.

Need for the Gospel

As sons of Adam and daughters of Eve, the Jews, like all other human beings, are dead in their trespasses and sins. Apart from Christ, they are utterly lost, like all the rest of us, and need to be converted to God if they are going to live forever with Him.

Romans 11

In Paul's illustration of the olive tree in Romans 11, he says that unbelieving Jews were cut out of the olive tree and that Gentile branches, wild olive branches, were grafted in (Rom. 11:17–29). This olive tree is the tree of the Abrahamic covenant. Paul's argument is that if the excision of the unbelieving Jews was such a great blessing to the Gentile world, what will their reintroduction be for the Gentiles but "life from the dead"? Thus many Reformed and Puritan theologians have for centuries thought that the conversion of the Jews *en masse* was the linchpin for the future evangelization of the world.

Supersessionism

Supersessionism is the belief that the Church is Israel now. All the promises of God are fulfilled in Christ, and

only there (2 Cor. 1:20). This means that the promises
given throughout the Old Testament are the present possession of Christians, not Jews. For the Jews to live under
these blessings, it is necessary for them to be grafted back
into the olive tree. Having said this, there is a distinction to be made between hard supersessionism and soft
supersessionism. Hard supersessionism believes that the
prediction made by Paul here was fulfilled in the first or
second century, and so there is no future "conversion of
the Jews" to look forward to. Modern ethnic Jews have
no unique standing with God at all, and must come to
Christ the same way that Swedes, Tibetans, Japanese,
and Argentinians must come. The soft supersessionists
are the ones who believe that the gifts and calling of God
are irrevocable, and that the natural olive branches, still
detached from the tree two thousand years later, are yet
to be grafted in again according to Paul's prediction. Soft
supersessionists believe that Jews are lost without Christ,
but believe that *as a people* they still have a role to play in
the history of redemption.

Talmudic Judaism

After the Temple was destroyed in AD 70, and the
Christian faith was firmly established as a going con-
cern by the second century, the rabbis who had not
turned to Jesus Christ had a problem. How were they
to maintain their distinctiveness from the Christians
when they no longer had a Temple, and hence could

not practice the Judaism of the Old Testament? Their solution to the problem was the development of what we now describe as Talmudic Judaism. The thing to emphasize for Christians is that this is *not* the religion of the Old Testament. There are many connections to the Old Testament, but this was a faith that came into existence after the time of Christ.

Zionism

Zionism is the belief that Jews have the right to live in their ancestral homeland, and that this homeland is roughly the territory of the modern state of Israel. Zionism as a movement began in the nineteenth century, when they had no territory, and their dream was realized in 1948, with the establishment of the state of Israel. When Zionism was first establishing itself, the claim was a scriptural one. This was their ancestral land—and it was a *de jure* claim, with them saying they had a right to the land. Whatever you make of that claim, Zionism is now a *de facto* reality, with millions of people living there on the basis of the earlier Zionist movement. This means that someone might live in Tel Aviv and not be a Zionist, and someone could be a Zionist and live in Brooklyn. These things can be complicated. I don't agree with Manifest Destiny, but I still live in Idaho. Suffice it to say that leftist antisemites are prepared to grant the claims to ancestral lands to pretty much anybody *except* the Jews.

APPENDIX 2

The Historic Reformed Position

AS A GENERAL RULE, THE REFORMED have not established eschatological doctrines as a point of division. There have been constant variations in what our theologians have affirmed over the centuries. But with that said, it also needs to be acknowledged that one of the broader currents in Reformed theology has been that of postmillennialism, and the conversion of the Jews was generally accepted as a key element of that doctrinal understanding. Though not universal, it was widespread—and among the Puritans, it was overwhelmingly widespread.

Iain Murray comments:

> Neither Luther nor Calvin saw a future general
> conversion of the Jews promised in Scripture; some
> of their contemporaries, however, notably Martin
> Bucer and Peter Martyr, who taught at Cambridge
> and Oxford respectively in the reign of Edward VI,
> did understand the Bible to teach a future calling
> of the Jews. In this view they were followed by
> Theodore Beza, Calvin's successor at Geneva.[1]

The fact that the conversion of the Jews was widely
accepted by our Reformed forefathers does not auto-
matically settle anything, but it ought to give us pause.
The point of this appendix is simply to give a representative sampling of this understanding, taken from
five centuries—the sixteenth, the seventeenth, the
eighteenth, the nineteenth, and the twentieth. And if
I really wanted to clinch the case, I could quote something that I wrote in the twenty-first. If I couldn't find
anything, I could just write something.

First, the sixteenth century. The Geneva Bible was
first published in 1560, and the editors of that work
expressed this view in the marginal notes for Romans
11:15 and 11:28. At verse 15, they say,

---

1. Iain H. Murray, *The Puritan Hope: Revival and the Interpretation of
Prophecy* (Edinburgh: The Banner of Truth Trust, 2014), 41.

It shall come to pass that when the Jews come to the Gospel, the world shall as it were come quicken again, and rise up from death to life.[2]

In the note for verse 28, they say,

Again, that he may join the Jews and Gentiles together as it were in one body, and especially may teach what duty the Gentiles owe to the Jews, he beateth this into their heads, that the nation of the Jews is not utterly cast off without hope of recovery.[3]

William Perkins was one of the leading Puritans during the Elizabethan era (dying in 1602), and he said this:

The Lord saith, *All the nations shall be blessed in Abraham*: Hence I gather that the nation of the Jews shall be called, and converted to the participation of this blessing: when, and how, God knows: but that it shall be done before the end of the world we know.[4]

In the seventeenth century, the Westminster Larger Catechism Question 191 asks what we pray for when we pray for the kingdom to come. Among other things,

2. 1599 Geneva Bible (White Hall, WA: Tolle Lege, 2011), 1155.
3. Ibid.
4. Murray, *The Puritan Hope*, 42.

we pray for "the gospel [to be] propagated throughout the world, the Jews called, [and] the fulness of the Gentiles brought in."

The Westminster Directory for the Public Worship of God does the same. It stipulates, in line with the Larger Catechism, that prayers be offered up "for the conversion of the Jews."

Some of the other men of this era who held to this view were John Owen, Thomas Manton, John Flavel, David Dickson, Jeremiah Burroughs, and James Durham.[5]

Richard Sibbes was also of this opinion:

> The Jews are not yet come in under Christ's banner; but God, that hath persuaded Japhet to come into the tents of Shem, will persuade Shem to come into the tents of Japhet, Gen. 9:27. The "fulness of the Gentiles is not yet come in," Rom. 11:25, but Christ, that hath the "utmost parts of the earth given him for his possession," Ps. 2:8, will gather all the sheep his Father hath given him into one fold, that there may be one sheepfold and one shepherd, John 10:16.[6]

Over here in America, Increase Mather wrote a book in 1669 entitled *The Mystery of Israel's Salvation Explained and Applied*. In that work, he wrote,

5. Murray, *The Puritan Hope*, 44.
6. Ibid., 43.

> That there shall be a general conversion of the
> Tribes of Israel is a truth which in some measure
> hath been known and believed in all ages of the
> Church of God, since the Apostles' days.... Only
> in these late days, these things have obtained
> credit much more universally than heretofore.[7]

The great Scottish theologian Samuel Rutherford, an emissary to the Westminster Assembly, said this in 1640:

> I shall be glad to be a witness, to behold the
> kingdoms of the world become Christ's. I could
> stay out of heaven many years to see that vic-
> torious triumphing Lord act that prophesied
> part of his soul-conquering love, in taking into
> his kingdom the greater sister, that kirk of the
> Jews, who sometime courted our Well-beloved
> for her little sister (Cant. 8.8); to behold him set
> up as an ensign and banner of love, to the ends
> of the world.[8]

Moving on to the next century, we come to Jonathan Edwards, one of the greatest theologians of

---

7. Increase Mather, *The Mystery of Israel's Salvation Explained and Applied*, Preface to the Reader and Proposition 5.6.

8. Murray, *The Puritan Hope*, 53–54.

the modern era. He was not at all ambiguous about his convictions.

> [The Jews] shall flow together to the blessed Jesus, penitently, humbly, and joyfully owning him as their glorious King and only Savior, and all with all their hearts, as with one heart and voice, declare his praises unto other nations. *Nothing is more certainly foretold than this national conversion of the Jews in Romans 11.* There are also many passages of the Old Testament which cannot be interpreted in any other sense, which I cannot now stand to mention.[9]

Another voice from the eighteenth century is that of Thomas Boston.

> There is a day coming when there shall be a national conversion of the Jews or Israelites. The now blinded and rejected Jews shall at length be converted into the faith of Christ, and join themselves to the Christian Church.... Have you any love to, or concern for the church, for the work of reformation, the reformation of our country, the reformation of our world? Any longing desire for the revival of that work now

9. Jonathan Edwards, *A History of the Work of Redemption,* in *The Works of Jonathan Edwards, Vol. 1* (Edinburgh: Banner of Truth Trust, 1976), 607.

at a stand; for a flourishing state of the church, that is now under a decay? Then pray for the conversion of the Jews.[10]

John Newton, author of "Amazing Grace," had this to add:

We have what may be called a standing miracle continually before our eyes; I mean the state of the Jews, who, though dispersed far and wide among many nations, are every where preserved a distinct and separate people. The history of the world affords no other instance of the like kind. The great monarchies, by which they were successively conquered and scattered, have successively perished. Only the names of them remain. But the people whom they despised, and endeavored to exterminate, subsist to this day; and, though sifted like corn over the earth, and apparently forsaken of God, are still preserved by his wonderful providence, unaffected by the changes and customs around them; still tenacious of the law of Moses, though the observance of it is rendered impracticable. Many days, many ages they have

10. Thomas Boston, "Encouragement to Pray for the Conversion of the Jews," in *The Whole Works of the Late Reverend Thomas Boston of Ettrick, Vol. 3*, ed. Samuel McMillan (Aberdeen: George and Robert King, 1848), 357–359.

lived as the prophets foretold they should, without a temple, without sacrifice or priest. (Hos. 3:4–5) As yet, many Heathen nations are permitted to walk in their own ways. But at length "the fulness of the Gentiles shall come in, and all Israel shall be saved." (Rom. 11:25–26) The revolutions and commotions in kingdoms and nations, which astonish and perplex politicians, are all bringing forward this great event.[11]

Entering the nineteenth century, the great Princeton theologian, Charles Hodge, also held this view.

The second great event, which, according to the common faith of the Church, is to precede the second advent of Christ, is *the national conversion of the Jews* ... That there is to be such a national conversion may be argued ... from the original call and destination of that people.[12]

He says the same in his commentary on Romans:

The simple meaning, therefore, of this verse is, that the future restoration of the Jews is, in itself, a

11. John Newton, *The Works of John Newton, Vol. 4*, ed. Richard Cecil (Edinburgh: The Banner of Truth Trust, 1985), 366–367.
12. Charles Hodge, *Systematic Theology, Vol. 3* (Grand Rapids, MI: Eerdmans, 1986), 805.

more probable event than the introduction of the
Gentiles into the church of God .... Having once
taken the Jews into special connection with himself, he never intended to cast them off forever.[13]

Robert Haldane agrees in his commentary on
Romans.

He now declares that at that period all Israel
shall be saved. The rejection of Israel has been
general, but at no period universal. This rejection
is to continue till the fullness of the Gentiles shall
come in. Then the people of Israel, as a body,
shall be brought to the faith of the Gospel. Such
expressions as that "all Israel shall be saved," are
no doubt, in certain situations, capable of limitation; but as no Scripture demands any limitation
of this expression, and as the opposition here
stated is between a *part* and *all* there is no war-
rant to make any exception, and with God this,
like all other things, is possible.[14]

We should also note the views of Charles Spurgeon,
the great Baptist preacher of the Victorian era.

13. Charles Hodge, *A Commentary on the Epistle to the Romans* (New York: A.C. Armstrong and Son, 1890), 583–584, 587.
14. Robert Haldane, *An Exposition of Romans* (Lafayette, IN: Sovereign Grace Publishers, 2001), 549.

I think we do not attach sufficient importance to the restoration of the Jews. We do not think enough of it. *But certainly, if there is anything promised in the Bible it is this....* The day shall yet come when the Jews, who were the first apostles to the Gentiles, the first missionaries to us who were afar off, shall be gathered in again.... *Matchless benefits to the world are bound up with the restoration of Israel; their gathering in shall be as life from the dead.*[15]

Coming into the twentieth century, R.C. Sproul said this:

So all Israel will be saved (v. 26a). If Paul is refer-ring to spiritual Israel, he is departing from the way he uses the term Israel here and in the pre-ceding three chapters. Since chapter 8 Paul has been talking about ethnic Israel. Does he mean each and every Jew? The word *all* in Scripture does not function the way we characteristically use it to indicate each and every. I believe Paul to be saying that the full complement of God's elect from Israel will be saved and that this will come in a new redemptive-historical visitation by the Holy Spirit when the time of the Gentiles is fulfilled.[16]

15. Murray, *The Puritan Hope*, 256.

16. R.C. Sproul, *Romans: An Expositional Commentary* (Sanford, FL: Reformation Trust Publishing, 2019), 353.

As for the twenty-first century, I will have to fulfill an earlier promise, and resort to something I said:

> For the time being, the Jews were enemies of the Gentile Christians, because of the gospel. But as concerns election, they are still beloved for their father's sake (v. 28). How long will this last? It is irrevocable, which is why the Jews will in fact return to Christ (v. 29).[17]

I don't know about you all, but I find this last quote strangely compelling.

---

17. Douglas Wilson, *To the Church in Rome* (Moscow, ID: Canon Press, 2022), 218.

APPENDIX 3

For Further Reading

THE OUTLOOK REPRESENTED BY THIS book is admittedly somewhat eclectic. If you want to read through the quarry where I obtained a bunch of this rock, I would recommend the following reading list, at least for a start. The books are ranked here alphabetically, according to the author's last name.

Robert Alter, *Pen of Iron*

Jerry Bowyer, *The Maker Versus the Takers*

Norman Finkelstein, *The Holocaust Industry*

George Gilder, *The Israel Test*

Yoram Hazony, *The Virtue of Nationalism*

215

Tom Hovestol, *Extreme Righteousness*

Peter Leithart, *From Silence to Song*

Bernard Lewis, *What Went Wrong?*

George McKenna, *The Puritan Origins of American Patriotism*

David Mitchell, *Messiah ben Joseph*

David Mitchell, *Jesus: The Incarnation of the Word*

Iain Murray, *The Puritan Hope*

Gary North, *The* Judeo-Christian *Tradition*

Charles Provan, *The Church Is Israel Now*

Jean Francois Revel, Anti-Americanism

Ethelbert Stauffer, *Christ and the Caesars*

Peter Zeihan, *The Accidental Superpower*

Now I said just above that the outlook of this book is eclectic, which a glance at these titles might indicate as well. If you were to read just one of these books, you might come away with one impression, and if you happened to choose another one, you could easily have an entirely different impression. I commend all the books to you, but not in a standalone fashion. George Gilder writes as a great admirer of Israel, and Robert Alter is a Jewish scholar who has noted the deep affinities that America has with the Jews, and Charles Proven is a strong supersessionist. Bernard Lewis writes about the Muslim world, but that is something that must be taken into account with all things Israel, and so forth.

All I ask is that you cut up all the vegetables, throw them all in the crockpot, and go away for the afternoon.